The Fire of Silence and Stillness

THE FIRE OF SILENCE
AND STILLNESS

An Anthology of Quotations for the
Spiritual Journey

edited by

PAUL HARRIS

Templegate Publishers
Springfield, Illinois

First published in 1995
by Darton, Longman and Todd Ltd
London

First published in 1996 in the United States of America
by Templegate Publishers
302 East Adams Street
P.O. Box 5152
Springfield, Illinois 62705

ISBN 0-87243-220-3
Library of Congress Catalog Card Number
95-62276

Cover photograph by Tim Woodcock

Contents

Acknowledgements

Close to half a century ago (1947 to be exact) I began to collect spiritual aphorisms and inspirational quotations in a ruled scribbler. That modest beginning was the origin and basis of the present compilation which has been greatly expanded to include contemporary spiritual writers from a broad range of religious traditions.

My special thanks go to a large number of publishers who have provided quotable words from over 200 authors on 'matters of the spirit.' I am especially grateful to the English book publisher Darton, Longman & Todd for permission to quote extensively from a variety of these authors, particularly John Main OSB and Bede Griffiths OSB. Thanks also to the same publisher for scriptural quotations from the Jerusalem Bible.

Whenever possible I have made an effort to identify and credit individual publishers with quotations in the Acknowledgements to Publishers section starting on page 217. However, some of the contributions in this anthology, dating back centuries, have proved impossible to trace to a specific published book. If, through inadvertence, any of these texts are copyrighted, I offer my apologies and seek the permission of any copyright holder.

This book is a not-for-profit project and any royalties will be spent on furthering the teaching of Christian meditation around the world.

My warm thanks to Carol Nixon for her word-processing expertise, Garrett Patterson for copy-editing assistance and Robert Kiely, Master of Adams House, Harvard University, Cambridge, Massachusetts, who assisted greatly in tracking sources of quotations. But most especially my thanks to Laurence Freeman, OSB, a member of Christ the King Benedictine Community, London, England and director of the World Community for Christian Meditation, who by his editorial advice and encouragement has made this book possible.

PAUL HARRIS
Editor

Preface

One of the great spiritual teachers of our time, the Benedictine monk Dom John Main (1926-82), was adamant that reading is no substitute for *experience*. In his talks on the spiritual path of Christian meditation (contemplative prayer) he cautioned that many of us, because of our intellectual orientation, substitute the reading of books and listening to talks on spirituality for the real thing. Meditation, he pointed out, is a discipline and what is important is to jump in daily and get wet, rather than to stand as an observer on the river-bank of prayer.

His point is well taken. No matter how avid our spiritual reading, it is all meaningless unless we put into practice the teaching inherent in the words meant to inspire us. Someone has pointed out that if we had to choose between a half-hour of silent meditation and hearing a lecture about it, most people would hunt for a good seat at the lecture.

But John Main was constantly quoting the words of Jesus, St Paul and other spiritual teachers. He obviously understood that insights from spiritual teachers and sages offer us a wealth of understanding and inspiration and make us heirs to the spiritual life of past ages. His talks continually drew on wide-ranging resources from St John of the Cross to the *New Yorker* magazine, from the fourth-century Desert Father John Cassian to the Indian sage Sri Ramakrishna.

The purpose therefore in editing this handbook of spiritual quotations was to select passages and aphorisms from the words of great spiritual teachers, including the accumulated wisdom of previous generations, that would assist pilgrims on their daily spiritual journey. The path of silence and stillness in prayer requires generosity, discipline, faith and commitment. This handbook is designed to give support and encouragement to all those on the journey. Not all of the quotations deal solely with the path of prayer: some of them are simply inserted to give an occasional jolt or spiritual shot in the arm.

7

As one can see from a cursory glance, no one age, culture or religious tradition has a monopoly on spiritual wisdom. In these pages we come to realize that the inner spiritual experience is everywhere in all ages the same: a longing for the Absolute in the silence of one's heart. The men and women quoted had a mission in common — to relate their particular time and culture to eternity and the things of the Spirit. Their prophetic voice rings out across the ages. I hope modern readers will bear with the noninclusive language of many of the older texts. It seemed best not to tamper with ancient quotations, which retain their original form in this anthology.

An anthology like this is meant to be read slowly, perhaps only one page at a time. It is intended primarily for daily readings. And if one is a follower of the path of silence and stillness in prayer, one will want to reflect on the readings as they speak to one's heart. The ideas, insights, perceptions and commentaries are meant to be read by the *heart* more than by the mind. As the spiritual classic *The Cloud of Unknowing* says: 'By love God may be grasped and held; by thought never.'

PAUL HARRIS
Ottawa, Canada

1
The Presence Within

Be still and know that I am God.

Psalm 46:10

The Kingdom of God does not come in such a way as to be seen. No one will say 'Look here it is!,' or 'There it is!' because the Kingdom of God is within you.

Luke 17:20-1

Heavenly Father,
Open my heart to the
Silent presence of
The spirit of your Son.
Lead me into that
Mysterious silence
Where your love is
Revealed to all who
Call.
MARANATHA

Come, Lord Jesus.

Dom John Main (1926-82)

It is truly the Christian's birthright to remain silent and recollected, like Mary of Bethany, in the Presence of the Father. This Presence is not, however, something outside one or separate from one, as when we see or imagine someone in front of us. It is rather a matter of entering inwardly within that unique Presence which fills time and eternity, the Presence of the Father to the Son and of the Son to the Father.

At the very heart of that glory and joy we hear the Thou which God in his love addresses to us from all eternity, and we no longer have the right to utter our own 'I' except within the Father's eternal I, where Being awakes to Itself.

> Henri Le Saux/Abhishiktananda (1910-73),
> *In Spirit and Truth*

In the very center of the cavern of the heart
  He, the Only One, He the Sole One,
I supreme, as a self supreme
In Himself self-luminous.

> Sri Ramana Maharshi (1879-1950)

Our real journey in life is interior: it is a matter of growth, deepening, and of an ever greater surrender to the creative action of love and grace in our hearts.

> Thomas Merton (1915-68),
> *The Road to Joy: Letters to New and Old Friends*

I think it is important to see that behind all the diversities of human nature there is a common ground and in that common ground every human being is in search of God, of ultimate meaning and ultimate truth. It is a solitary search, because it touches the depth of our being and it is something which no one else can give us.

All of us human beings have a capacity for God, a capacity to be drawn by God into the depths of our being where we experience the presence of God, of the infinite, eternal reality that sustains the world as the ground and source of our being.

> Bede Griffiths (1907-93),
> *The New Creation in Christ*

Utterly at home, He lives in us for ever.

Julian of Norwich (1342-1420),
The Joy of the Saints

The vision of
The unseen and
The confidence
That comes from
Being absorbed
In the immortal,
Is what meditation
Is about.

Dom John Main (1926-82),
in conversation

In the center of the castle of Brahman, our own body, there is a small shrine in the form of a lotus flower, and within can be found a small space. We should find who dwells there and we should want to know him. And if anyone asks: 'Who is he who dwells in a small shrine in the form of a lotus flower in the center of the castle of Brahman?' we can answer: 'The little space within the heart is as great as the universe. The heavens and earth are there, the sun, the moon, the stars; fire and lightning and winds; for the whole universe is in him and he dwells within our heart.'

Chandogya Upanishad

Accompanied by none
Singing my song of solitude
May I approach Him who dwells
In the cave of my heart.
And make this journey of mine
A journey into my own inner death.

Vadakethala F. Vineeth,
Songs of Solitude

When I entered into Thy depth,
Oh! what happened to me?
Oh! what happened to Thee?

When I entered into Thy depth,
there remained no longer either Thou or I!

Sri Gnanananda

When one enters the deeper layers of contemplative prayer one sooner or later experiences the void, the emptiness, the nothingness, the darkness, the unknowing, the profound mystical silence. All these words point to the same reality. Yet, it is as though there is within me an immense and bottomless void. And when one first experiences this void there is an absence of thought and imaginative pictures, and perhaps there is a certain forgetfulness, as forms are buried beneath a cloud of forgetting.

'Nothing, nothing, nothing, and even on the mountain nothing.' But the nothing is all; the emptiness is fullness, the void is plentitude. To experience the vast inner nothing is to experience the vast inner all. It is to experience the 'eternal now.' This is the doctrine of St John of the Cross and the whole apophatic tradition which he represents...

As this emptiness deepens, one carries it around always — when one is talking and laughing and teaching and walking and standing on the train. It is there when one goes to sleep at night and when one awakens in the morning. At first the void is frightening, terribly frightening, as one loses all security; but later it becomes a spring of clear water welling up to life eternal and giving great joy. This is because one comes to realise that the void has a source: and the source is Jesus, the Word Incarnate, the Inner Guest. And he is opening up the way to an even more immense and limitless and bottomless void which is the Father.

William Johnston,
Letters to Contemplatives

God's chief aim is giving birth.
He is never content till he begets his Son in us.

Meister Eckhart (1260-1327),
Sermons and Treatises

To pray is to descend with the mind into the heart, and there to stand before the face of the Lord — ever-present, all-seeing, within you.

Bishop Theophane the Recluse (1815-94),
The Art of Prayer: An Orthodox Anthology

God loves us too much to allow us to be satisfied and contented with mere images or signs of his Presence, like the material icons that we see or the mental concepts of him that we form with our intelligence. It is to his most secret and hidden abode — symbolised by the clouds which covered Mount Sinai or enveloped Jesus at his Ascension — that God calls his beloved children. The words of Jesus in the Gospel exactly express the Father's will: 'Father, I desire that they also…may be with me where I am' (John 17:24).

Henri Le Saux/Abhishiktananda (1910-73),
Prayer

That which is at the centre of the space
    in my heart
it is the very same which is in the sun,
which is in the earth,
in the heart of every man
at the heart of every being.

Chandogya Upanishad

You dwell there in my heart,
store-house of the secrets which come
    from you;
you are welcome to abide here!

13

Within there is no longer any but you,
supreme mystery whose presence I divine.
Look now with your own eyes;
is there an intruder in the house?

Al-Hallaj (858-922)

Let yourself
be plumbed to the depths,
and you will realise
that everyone
is created for a presence.
There, in your heart of hearts,
in that place
where no two people
are alike,
Christ is waiting for you.
And there
the unexpected happens.

Roger Schutz,
A Life We Never Dared Hope For

For, though God be everywhere present, yet He is only present
to thee in the deepest and most central part of thy soul. Thy natural
sense cannot possess God or unite thee to him; nay, thy inward
faculties of understanding, will, and memory, can only reach after
God, but cannot be the place of his habitation in thee.

But there is a root or depth in thee from whence all these
faculties come forth, as lines from a centre or as branches from
the body of the tree. This depth is called the Centre, the Fund or
Bottom of the soul. This depth is the unity, the eternity, I had
almost said the infinity of thy soul; for it is so infinite that nothing
can satisfy it or give it any rest but the infinity of God.

William Law (1686-1761),
The Classics of Western Spirituality

Try to enter
the treasure chamber

14

that is within you
and then you discover
the treasure chamber
of heaven.
They are one and the same.
If you succeed
in entering one,
you will see both.

St Isaac of Syria (sixth century),
taken from *The Joy of the Saints*

However well of Christ
you talk and preach
unless he lives within,
he is beyond your reach.

Angelus Silesius (1624-77),
The Enlightened Heart

There is in the heart... 'the peace of God that passeth all understanding,' a quietness and confidence which is the source of all
strength, a sweet peace, 'which nothing can offend,' a deep rest
which the world can neither give nor take away. There is in the
center of the soul a chamber of peace where God dwells, and
where, if we will only enter and hush every other sound, we will
hear His still small voice.

There is in the swiftest wheel that revolves on its axis, a place
in the very center where there is no movement at all; and so in the
busiest life there is a place where we can dwell alone with God in
eternal stillness. There is only one way to know God, 'Be still and
know.' God is in His holy temple, let the earth keep silence before
Him.

C.E. Cowman,
Streams in the Desert

Deep, deep down,
in the total darkness
of the Cave,

15

is a Flame,
a solitary Flame!
Who will ever tell the secret
which the Flame hides
at its heart?
He alone will learn the secret —
a secret he can never share —
who, once fallen into that Flame,
and swallowed up,
remains henceforth
nothing but Flame!

Upanishads

Contemplation is not a means to an end. It is not even a goal sought for itself. It is so utterly simple that the very desire for it becomes an obstacle to achieving it. And when you achieve it, you haven't really achieved anything. You do not get some place where you were not. You are getting where you always really are: in the presence of God. You have achieved nothing. Yet you have achieved everything. For you have been transformed in consciousness so that at last you recognize yourself for who you really are.

William H. Shannon,
Seeking the Face of God

O beauty ever ancient, ever new.
Too late have I loved you.
I was outside and you were within me.
And I never found you until I found
You within myself.

St. Augustine (354-430),
The Classics of Western Spirituality

We do not need to go to Calcutta to find Christ in the poor. If we have not found Him in our very midst, if we have not learned to love those who share our daily lives more than ourselves, preferring their needs to ours, then we will not find Him anywhere else. As Mother Teresa has said: 'Do not search for Christ in far off

16

lands. He is not there. He is in you.'

We find Christ in every moment which is truly present to us and we to it. The present moment is, therefore, always the moment of Christ. Our neighbour is, therefore, always the present Christ. Saying the mantra restrains our ego and roots us in the present; likewise turning to the poorest of our neighbours restrains our egoism and shatters our illusions, revealing to us the only wisdom we can hope to acquire — the wisdom of humility. Humility is to be grounded in the truth about ourselves — that we are poor.

Lee-Moy Teresa Ng
'Meditation and working among the poor'

If anyone loves me he will keep my word, and my Father will love him, and we shall come to him and make our home with him.

John 14:23

Prayer is about
        seeking God
    in the stillness
beyond words or thought.
    It is about awakening
to the presence of God within us.

Laurence Freeman

A great many people think their body is themselves. Others think the personality is themselves. 'This personality is me, this is my self,' and so they are satisfied.

Others reflect that this personality of mine — my thoughts, feelings, desires — is going to pass away when my body decays. This is not the self I am seeking, for it belongs to the changing world.

The basic orientation of the Upanishads is found in the search for the inner self, the self beyond the body and the mind.

This is a hidden mystery. We look into the depths of our being and find this hidden mystery. In Christian terms you have discovered yourself in God. In the words of St Paul in Ephesians 3, *The mystery long hidden is revealed, it is Christ in you, the hope of glory.*

Bede Griffiths (1907-93),
The Universal Christ

In the midst of the cave of the heart,
in the form of the I, in form of the Self,
unique and solitary,
Brahman's glory shines
directly from Himself on Himself.
Penetrate deep within,
your thought piercing to its source,
your mind having plunged into itself,
with breath and sense held close in the
    depths, your whole self fixed in yourself,
and there, simply BE!

Sri Ganarati Sastri

There is a Light that shines beyond all things on earth, beyond us all, beyond the heavens, beyond the highest, the very highest heavens. This is the Light that shines in our heart.

Chandogya Upanishad

One 2 June 1952 he noted in his Journal: It is not a question of attaining to the knowledge of God or to the Presence of God, but of recognizing, realizing, that this Presence *is.*

Henri Le Saux/Abhishiktananda (1910-73),
The Secret of Arunachala

Enter into yourself
to the place where there is nothing,
and take care that nothing enters there.
Penetrate within yourself
to the place where there is no more any
    thought,

18

and take care that no thought arises there!

There where there is nothing —
Fullness!
There where nothing is seen —
the Vision of Being!
There where nothing more appears —
behold, the Self!

That is dhyana!

Sri Gnanananda

The all-important aim in Christian meditation is to allow God's mysterious and silent presence within us to become more and more not only a reality, but *the* reality in our lives; to let it become that reality which gives meaning and shape and purpose to everything we do; to everything we are.

Dom John Main (1926-82)
Word into Silence

God is not an idea,
    or a definition
    that we have
    committed to memory;

    he is a presence
    which we experience
    in our hearts.

Louis Evely,
The Gospels without Myth

Make your home in me as I make mine in you. As a branch cannot bear fruit all by itself but must remain part of the vine, neither can you unless you remain in me. I am the vine, you are the branches. Whoever remains in me, with me in him, bears fruit in plenty.

John 15:4-5

I honor in you
that place in you
where the Lord resides

And when you
are in that place
in you

And I am
in that place
in me

Then there is
only one of us.

Ancient Indian prayer: 'Namaste'

If we go down into ourselves, we find that we possess exactly
what we desire.

Simone Weil (1909-43),
Waiting for God

God is
the transcendent mystery
at the core
of human history,
the deepest dimension
of human life...
who calls us...
and graces us...
to become more fully human....

The inner gesture
of prayer therefore [is]...
the attempt to be...
more reflectively present
to what happens every day...

20

an attempt to be in touch with
the root of one's personal existence
and the mystery alive
in the community.

Gregory Baum,
Are We Losing the Faith?

In the Hindu tradition the Upanishads speak of the spirit of the One who created the universe as dwelling in our heart. The same spirit is described as the One who in silence is loving to all. In our own Christian tradition Jesus tells us of the Spirit who dwells in our heart and the Spirit as the Spirit of love.

Dom John Main (1926-82),
Moment of Christ

This same atman which is within the heart
is greater than the sky and greater than
    the earth
greater than all the worlds...
it contains all works, all desires,
all scents, and likewise all tastes;
it fills the entire universe,
this atman at the center of my heart,
it is Brahman itself.

Chandogya Upanishad

I stand at the door and knock. If you respond to my voice and open the door, I will enter your space and share your food; and you will share with me.

Revelation 3:20

Christ...a fire capable of penetrating everything — and which little by little, spreads everywhere.

Pierre Teilhard de Chardin (1881-1955),
The Divine Milieu

21

Dwell, O mind, within yourself;
Enter no other's home.
If you but seek there, you will find
All you are searching for.
God, the true Philosopher's Stone,
Who answers every prayer,
Lies hidden deep within your heart,
The richest gem of all.
How many pearls and precious stones
Are scattered all about
The outer court that lies before
The chamber of your heart!

Songs of Sri Ramakrishna (1836-86)

In the inner person dwells God, the Truth, who cannot be reached by those who seek him in externals. God, whose nature it is to be always and only within and in the most inward place.

Meister Eckhart (1260-1327),
Sermons and Treatises

When you seek God, seek Him in your heart. He is not in Jerusalem, not in Mecca nor in the Hajj.

Yunus Emre (1280-1330)

Her heart is full of joy with love,
For in the Lord her mind is stilled,
She has renounced every selfish attachment
And draws abiding joy and strength
From the One within.
She lives not for herself, but lives
To serve the Lord of Love in all,
And swims across the sea of life
Breasting its rough waves joyfully.

St Teresa of Avila (1515-82),
'Her heart is full of joy'

All of a sudden I perceived that in the silence was a presence. At the heart of the silence there was He who is all stillness, all peace, all poise.

Georges Bernanos (1888-1948)

December 1956 The joy of Christmas, you know, is not only the creche. The creche is just a sign. It is into the cave within the heart that we should go to hide ourselves, lose ourselves, forget ourselves. This is the true cave where Jesus is born in us, and being born in us makes us into himself. This cave is the bosom of the eternal Father, where the Word is born and comes to be from all eternity.

Our joy at Christmas, joy in the family, joy in worship, etc., all that is so little beside the true joy, the joy of Jesus awaking to being that night in Bethlehem, the joy of the divine Word awaking to being in the bosom of the Father in eternity! Live in this cave in the depth of your heart, that mystery into which India has penetrated so deeply.

Henri Le Saux/Abhishiktananda (1910-73),
His Life Told through his Letters

Prayer is loving attentiveness to the mystery within us.

Dom John Main (1926-82)
Word into Silence

Heaven is hidden in the depth of the heart, that glorious place which is only found by those who renounced themselves.

Mahanarayana Upanishad

God is the still point at the centre. There is no doer but he. All this he showed me with great joy, saying 'See, I am God. See, I am in all things. See, I do all things.'

Julian of Norwich (1342-1420),
Daily Readings with Julian of Norwich

I abide in this secret place in the depth of my heart, there —
where all alone before God I am,
where all alone with God I am,
where all alone from God I am,
where alone is He who Is.

Henri Le Saux/Abhishiktananda (1910-73),
Ermites Du Saccidananda

All that matters is to be at one with the living God
to be a creature in the house of the God of life.

Like a cat asleep on a chair
at peace, in peace
and at one with the master of the house, with the mistress,
at home, at home in the house of the living,
sleeping on the hearth, and yawning before the fire.

Sleeping on the hearth of the living world
yawning at home before the fire of life
feeling the presence of the living God
like a great reassurance
a deep calm in the heart
a presence
as of the master sitting at the board
in his own and greater being,
in the house of life.

D.H. Lawrence (1885-1930),
The Enlightened Heart

2
The Kingdom of Heaven

Faith is the substance of things to be hoped for, the evidence of things not seen.

Hebrews 11:1

One evening I heard some music from a distant concert, and the thought came that soon I shall be listening to the sweet melodies of heaven. This thought, however, gave me only a moment's joy, for one hope alone makes my heart beat fast — the love I shall receive and the love I shall be able to give!

I feel that my mission is soon to begin — to make others love God as I love him...to teach souls my little way. I will spend my heaven doing good on earth. This is not impossible, for the angels in heaven watch over us. No, there can be no rest for me till the end of the world, till the angel shall have said 'Time is no more' (Revelation 10:6). Then I shall take my rest, then I shall be able to rejoice, because the number of the elect will be complete.

St Thérèse of Lisieux (1873-97),
Daily Readings with St. Thérèse

For the gate is narrow and the way is hard, that leads to life, and those who find it are few.

Matthew 7:14

There is a reality even prior to heaven and
    earth;
Indeed, it has no form, much less a name;
Eyes fail to see it;
It has no voice for ears to detect...
It is not mind, nor Buddha;
Absolutely quiet, and yet illuminating in
    a mysterious way,
It allows itself to be perceived only by
    the clear-eyed.

Dai-o Kokushi,
On Zen

The kingdom of heaven is like a mustard seed which a man took
and sowed in his field. It is the smallest of all seeds, but when it
has grown it is the biggest shrub of all and becomes a tree so that
the birds of the air come and shelter in its branches.

Matthew 13:31-2

We must be saved together. We must come to God together.
Together we must all return to our Father's house. What would
God say to us if some of us came to Him without the others?

Charles Péguy (1873-1914)

Make ready
for the
Christ
whose
smile, like
lightning
sets free
the song of
everlasting
glory
that now
sleeps, in
your

26

paper
flesh, like
dynamite.

Thomas Merton (1915-68)

At this time the disciples came to Jesus and said, 'Who is the greatest in the kingdom of heaven?' So he called a little child to him and set the child in front of them. Then he said, 'I tell you solemnly, unless you change and become like little children you will never enter the kingdom of heaven. And so, the one who makes himself as little as this little child is the greatest in the kingdom of heaven.'

Matthew 18:1-4

I have come so that they may have life and have it to the full.

John 10:10

Let not him who seeks cease until he finds, and when he finds he shall be astonished. Astonished he shall reach the Kingdom, and having reached the Kingdom, he shall rest....

And the Kingdom of heaven is within you and whosoever knoweth himself shall find it. And, having found it, ye shall know yourselves that ye are sons and heirs of the Father, the Almighty, and shall know yourselves that ye are in God and God in you. And ye are the City of God.

F.C. Happold (1893-1971),
Oxyrhynchus Sayings of Jesus on Mysticism

Those who live in the Lord never see each other for the last time.

German proverb

Begin to search and dig in thine own field for this pearl of eternity that lies hidden in it; it cannot cost thee too much, nor canst thou buy it too dear, for it is all; and when thou hast found it thou wilt know that all which thou hast sold or given away for it is as mere a nothing as a bubble upon the water.

William Law (1686-1761),
The Classics of Western Spirituality

Love Was
without
beginning
Is
and
Shall Be
without
ending.

Julian of Norwich (1342-1420),
Daily Readings with Julian of Norwich

You have died and your life is hidden with Christ in God.

Colossians 3:3

To find our own centre is the reverse of becoming self-centred. It is to awaken to the centre beyond ourselves, whence we are created and to which we return with Christ, the centre where we find ourselves and Him in that experience of communion we call the Kingdom.

Dom John Main (1926-82),
The Present Christ

The recovery of the contemplative dimension of our lives, therefore, goes far beyond a change in behaviour. It is nothing less than a spiritual revolution that awakens deep levels of consciousness in us: not just the surface consciousness of our superficial self, but the inner depth consciousness of our real self, which we experience as nothing apart from the Being of God.

It is what the Fathers of the Church, especially the Eastern Fathers, like to call the discovery of the heart: the heart, not as a physical organ, but as the center of my being, the place where I am most truly myself, the place where I experience God, the place where I find my brothers and sisters in an entirely new way.

William Shannon,
Seeking the Face of God

The kingdom of heaven is like treasure hidden in a field, which a man found and covered up; then in his joy he goes and sells all that he has and buys that field. Again, the kingdom of heaven is like a merchant in search of fine pearls, who, on finding one pearl of great value, went and sold all that he had and bought it.

Matthew 13:44-6

3
The Fruits of Prayer

Sitting....Sitting
And the grass grows greener.

Zen Buddhist meditation saying

Thomas Aquinas, himself a Dominican friar, has more esteem for
action as it appears in what he calls the mixed life. This is the
overflow of mysticism: sharing the fruits of contemplation with
others. For Thomas this is the more perfect life for two reasons.
Firstly, because it is better for the candle to give light than just to
burn, and in the same way it is better to share the fruit of
contemplation than just to contemplate. Secondly, this mixed life
was chosen by Jesus Christ — who taught and preached and healed
and lived an active life.

For Thomas, then, the eye of love gazes not only on divine
realities but also on human realities. Or, more correctly, it sees
the divine in the human: it sees God in the world. Mysticism
overflows into activity.

William Johnston,
The Inner Eye of Love

Christ has no body now on earth but yours,
no hands but yours,

30

no feet but yours,
Yours are the eyes through which is to look out
  Christ's compassion to the world;
Yours are the feet with which he is to
  go about doing good;
Yours are the hands with which he is to
  bless men now.

St Teresa of Avila (1515-82),
'You are Christ's hands'

The world is charged with the grandeur of God.

Gerard Manley Hopkins (1844-89),
Everyman's Book of Victorian Verse

The righteous flourish like the palm tree,
And grow like a cedar in Lebanon...
They still bring forth fruit in old age,
They are ever full of sap and green...

Psalm 92:12, 14

Yet I remain a contemplative. I do not think there is a contradiction for I think at least some contemplatives must try to understand the providential events of the day. God works in history; therefore a contemplative who has no sense of history, no sense of historical responsibility, is not fully a Christian contemplative: he is gazing at God as a static essence, or as an intellectual light, or as a nameless ground of being. But we are face to face with the Lord of History and with Christ the King and Savior, the Light of the World....

We must confront Him in the awful paradoxes of our day, in which we see that society is being judged. And in all this we have to retain a balance and a good sense which seem to require a miracle, and yet they are the fruit of ordinary grace. In a word we have to continue to be Christians in all the full dimensions of the Gospel.

Thomas Merton (1915-68),
The Hidden Ground of Love

Jesus is the man who is totally given to God, to the Father, the one who is totally surrendered to the vertical movement, so that the son always sees what the Father is doing. At the same time he was totally open to all people and to life as a whole. That is the dual movement, vertical and horizontal, of contemplation in action, action in contemplation.

This is a universal call not only for monks or for nuns or for unmarried people but for everybody who seeks God.

Bede Griffiths (1907-93),
The Universal Christ

I expect nothing of myself but everything of God.

St Thérèse of Lisieux (1873-94)
Autobiography of St Thérèse of Lisieux

I have placed you in the midst of your fellows that you may do to them what you cannot do to me, that is to say that you may love your neighbor of free grace without expecting any return from him, and what you do to him I count as done to me.

from the dialogue of
St Catherine of Siena (1347-80)

The love which we bear to others remains the mark of the authenticity of our contemplation.

Roger Schutz

To see a world in a grain of sand
And heaven in a wild flower,
Hold infinity in the palm of your hand
And eternity in an hour.

William Blake (1757-1827)

The warmth that is provided by our capacity to love is as necessary for the soul's growth as any other part of the meditational way. It radiates from our efforts to express love to those both at home and farther away. It comes from our acceptance of others as they are, from learning to listen to them and becoming sensitive to their needs. It increases as we look out for the strangers and welcome them, and particularly as we work at trying to transform our enemies into friends.

Steadily the warmth that is given this kind of action draws the soul toward the reality of the loving God. Step by step the soul's reach grows, so that it becomes easier to find the One who is Love through meditation and to carry more of His love out actively to others.

> Morton Kelsey,
> *The Other Side of Silence*

The only way to measure growth in prayer is by a qualitative change in one's life.

> Dom John Main (1926-82),
> in conversation

Prayer which does not have direct human and social application is not Christian prayer.

Merton held that solitude and interior prayer were closely linked with the awakening of the social conscience.... It is in the solitude, in the depths of a person's own aloneness, that there lie the resources for resistance to injustice....

For Merton the understanding of prayer is crucial to the understanding of social change. There is no split between spirituality and social responsibility. The time will shortly be upon us, if it is not already here, when the pursuit of contemplation becomes a strictly subversive activity.

> Daniel Berrigan

The great grace that all of us have been given to believe in Jesus Christ, to believe in His presence in our hearts.... That is an extraordinary gift to have been given. We have to learn, because

it is a gift of such staggering proportions, to respond to it
gradually, gently...we cannot understand the sheer magnificence
and wonder of it.

Dom John Main (1926-82),
Community of Love

The poverty of the way of meditation can enable us to be open to
the challenge of the poor, to allow ourselves to be touched by their
suffering, to be vulnerable. The protective layers of our ego
gradually disappear as we acknowledge their presence and recog-
nise that we do not really need to protect ourselves in this way.

Often we meditate in the midst of a busy day, perhaps in a
climate that is hot and humid with the loud and constant cry of our
Muslim neighbours coming through the loud speaker that is
directed towards our house! This prayer can be an experience of
real poverty, emptiness. Yet, to remain faithful to the twice-daily
meditation somehow transforms us at the deepest level of our
being. There we know poverty but it is — to use the phrase of
Cassian — the grand poverty of the mantra. When we are poor,
then we are rich.

Sister Maura Ramsbottom,
'Meditation and mission'

The contemplative who can stand back from a situation and see it
for what it is, is more threatening to an unjust social system than
the frenzied activist who is so involved in the situation that he
cannot see clearly at all.

Karl Barth (1881-1966),
Karl Barth Reader

Our prayer life and our actions.... The two cannot be separated
for they are of the same fabric. What we do with our lives
outwardly, how well we care for others, is as much a part of
meditation as what we do in quietness and turning inward. In fact,
Christian meditation that does not make a difference in the quality
of one's outer life is short-circuited. It may flare for a while, but
unless it results in finding richer and more loving relationships

with other human beings or in changing conditions in the world that cause human suffering, the chances are that an individual's prayer activity will fizzle out.

Morton Kelsey,
The Other Side of Silence

And finally the journey into the castle propels one back into the world. This is the reason for prayer, my daughters, the purpose of this spiritual marriage; the birth always of good works, good works.

St Teresa of Avila (1515-82),
The Collected Works of St Teresa of Avila

In Paul there was no schizophrenic cleavage between his relationship with God and his relationships with people. It was all one. Life was flowing into his prayer as his prayer flowed into life.

Finally, as life flows into prayer, so prayer must flow into life. The loving presence of God experienced in mystical prayer can be experienced also in the hurly-burly of life. The anguishing absence of God experienced in mystical prayer can be experienced in the hurly-burly of life. This is the ideal of contemplation in action.

William Johnston,
Christian Mysticism Today

One must guard against self-deception with regard to the contemplative experience. An ever-present danger in the life of the contemplative is the intrusion of a narcissistic preoccupation with self. The end of such a detour is a self-indulgence that is indifferent to others. Such an attitude is a religious twin to the hyperindividualism of self-centred materialism. It is a form of religious fundamentalism that focuses on personal salvation and ignores the human family.

Thomas Merton labels such pseudo-contemplation as idolatry, as seductive as any imaginable, with ruin an almost inevitable end. A lack of concern for the world or an inability to 'bear the burden of others' and share in their suffering is a sign that one shares neither the mind nor the heart of God.

Raymond Bailey,
Thomas Merton on Mysticism

That evening after sunset they brought to him all who were ill or possessed by devils; and the whole town was there, gathered at the door. He healed many who suffered from various diseases.... Very early next morning he got up and went out. He went away to a lonely spot and remained there in prayer.

Mark 1:32-4, 35

Imagine a circle with its centre and radii or rays going out from this centre. The further these radii are from the centre the more widely are they dispersed and separated from one another; and conversely, the closer they come to the centre, the closer they are to one another. Suppose now that this circle is the world, the very centre of the circle, God, and the lines (radii) going from the centre to the circumference or from the circumference to the centre are the paths of men's lives. Then here we see the same.

In so far as the saints move inwards within the circle towards its centre, wishing to come near to God, then, in the degree of their penetrations, they come closer both to God and to one another; moreover, inasmuch as they come nearer to God, they come nearer to one another, and inasmuch as they come nearer to one another, they come nearer to God.

Abba Dorotheus (seventh century),
Early Fathers from the Philokalia

In the final analysis meditation is a love affair. And love is the most powerful energy in the universe. The great irony of meditation is that we become more immersed in the here-and-now. We are liberated from our false egos, and begin to know and love others at a deeper level of awareness. Liberated from our possessiveness we reach out with a new found compassion to our family, friends, and the less fortunate.

William Johnston,
Silent Music

This is how we know what love is: Christ gave his life for us. We too, then, ought to give our lives for our brothers! If a rich person sees his brother in need, yet closes his heart against his brother, how can he claim that he loves God? My children, our love should not be just words and talk; it must be true love, which shows itself in action.

1 John 3:16-18

Teresa of Avila's life shows us that this matching of vision by action means more than putting theory into practice within. There is her vision of watering the soul's garden, of journeying from mansion to mansion to the luminous center of the Interior Castle. And outwardly there is her entanglement in Church politics, in fighting and intrigue. The two seem worlds apart, at first sight.

She was not shown a blueprint for reforming the Carmelites, ready to be carried out. That is not how contemplation works. She simply exposed her heart to the radiance of 'the temple not built by human hands.' And in its light it became clear to her, step by step, where the building of the temple here below needed a helping hand. That she was obedient to that vision was what made her the great contemplative.

David Steindl-Rast,
Gratefulness the Heart of Prayer

Interior growth is only possible when we commit ourselves with and to others.

Jean Vanier

It is known to many that we need solitude to find ourselves. Perhaps it is not so well known that we need solitude to find our fellows. Even the Saviour is described as reaching mankind through the wilderness.

Havelock Ellis (1859-1939)

Every man or woman who practises this work will find that it so suffuses body and soul, as to make them gracious and attractive to everyone who sees them.

Indeed, if the least attractive man or woman were drawn by grace to work in this way, their appearance would be quickly changed to one of such graciousness, that all good people who saw them would be glad and happy to have them in their company, and would know that in God's grace they were cheered and strengthened by their presence.

Therefore get this gift — all who by grace may do so. Whoever truly has it will know how to rule himself and all that is his.

He will be wise and perceptive in discerning the character of others. It enables him to be at ease with all who would speak to him — 'saints' and 'sinners' alike — without being drawn into sin himself; and all this to the astonishment of those who see him, and at the same time drawing them through grace to the work in which he is being formed.

Anon (fourteenth century),
The Cloud of Unknowing

There can be no perfect virtue, none that bears fruit, unless it be exercised by means of our neighbour.

St. Catherine of Siena (1347-80),
The Classics of Western Spirituality

If you do away with the yoke, the clenched fist, the wicked word, if you give your bread to the hungry, and relief to the oppressed, your light will rise in darkness and your shadows become like noon. Yahweh will give strength to your bones, and you shall be like a watered garden, like a spring of water which never runs dry.

Isaiah 58:9-11

My answer is meditation; I do not know any other way of discovering this inner harmony. If a person learned to sit and meditate and allowed the body and the mind to become calm, then the deeper level of the spirit would emerge.

Bede Griffiths (1907-93),
in conversation

> The Spirit produces
> love, joy, peace,
> patience, kindness,
> goodness, faithfulness,
> humility and self-control

Galatians 5:22, 23a

Social action should flow from our contemplation. It should not be a sideline or something inherently different, but should be integrated in our prayer and meditation.

Personally, I have always found that unless meditation is fed by concern with people's problems and the world's problems it loses its depth. There is no rivalry between contemplation and action. There is a danger when people feel that because the world's problems are so demanding they must give their whole life to the poor in action.

I remember a friend who joined a team working with the poor in Brazil. Their idea was that there was no need for Mass or prayer because Christ was in the poor. One had only to go out to the poor and one would meet Christ in them. So they gave up Mass and prayer and concentrated only on active service to the poor. Within a few years the work totally disintegrated. I think unless we find Christ within, we will not find him among the poor, though we may be doing good to them in various ways. The two are reciprocal: the more we find Christ within, the more we become aware of Christ without. There is a polarity here, one acting on the other.

Bede Griffiths (1907-93),
The New Creation in Christ

I see His blood upon the rose
and in the stars the glory of his eyes.

Joseph Mary Plunkett (1887-1916),
World's Great Religious Poetry

Love is the synthesis of contemplation and action, the meeting-point between heaven and earth, between God and man.

I have known the satisfaction of unrestrained action, and the joy of the contemplative life in the dazzling peace of the desert, and I repeat again St Augustine's words: 'Love and do as you will.' Don't worry about what you ought to do. Worry about loving. Don't interrogate heaven repeatedly and uselessly saying, 'What course of action should I pursue?' Concentrate on loving instead.

And by loving you will find out what is for you. Loving, you will listen to the Voice. Loving, you will find peace.

Love is the fulfilment of the law and should be everyone's rule of life; in the end it's the solution to every problem, the motive for all good.

'Love and do as you will.'

Carlo Carretto (1910-89),
Letters from the Desert

I discover more and more each day my need for these times of solitude in which I can rediscover others with more truth, and accept in the light of God my own weakness, ignorance, egoism and fear. This solitude does not separate me from others: it helps me love them more tenderly, realistically and attentively. I begin to distinguish between the false solitude which is a flight from others to be alone with egoism, sadness and a bruised sensitivity, and true solitude which is a communion with God and others.

Jean Vanier,
Community and Growth

There is something incomplete about contemplation if it is not shared. That is why heaven, where the ultimate perfection of contemplation will be achieved, will not be a place of separate

40

individuals, each with his own private vision of God; rather, it will be a sea of Love flowing through the One Person of all the elect.

William H. Shannon,
Thomas Merton's Dark Path

Perhaps in the beginning of our spiritual journey we placed an emphasis on the difference between daily activities with others and our time alone in prayer. It is true that no amount of prayer can ever take the place of loving and being loved by others, just as loving and being loved by others cannot take the place of prayer.

At the same time, however, we discover that in fidelity to prayer and loving and being loved by others, the lines of demarcation between these two spheres break down. The union with God we seek in prayer embraces us unexpectedly in a moment of simply being with another person. And in a moment of solitary prayer we are granted a sudden awareness of another with a heightened capacity to love that person, to accept him or her in the compassion that holds us in our prayer.

James Finley,
The Awakening Call

As a society, we are closing down our life support systems. This is terrifying. But there is hope that this can be turned around. As Thomas Berry points out, it is necessary for the human community and the earth community to go into the future as a single sacred community. And I think it is important to recognize that while we are distinct from the Ground of Love, we are not separate. Then we realize our unity and communion with every human being, with the earth and with the universe. Let us not undervalue our great work, the work of meditation.

Charles Brandt,
Christian Meditation by Those Who Practice It

Is the Christian life of prayer simply an evasion of the problems and anxieties of contemporary existence?...If we pray 'in the Spirit' we are certainly not running away from life, negating visible reality in order to 'see God.' For 'the Spirit of the Lord has filled the whole earth.' Prayer does not bind us to the world, but it transforms our vision of the world, and make us see it, all people, all the history of humankind in the light of God.

Thomas Merton (1915-68),
The Climate of Monastic Prayer

The personal fruits of prayer include love, joy, peace, patience, kindness, goodness, gentleness and self-control. But these fruits often also include a call to action. The flame of love that springs from prayer can suddenly burst forth. Like the prophets of old, the person of prayer often has an inner eye awakened to suffering and injustice in the world and suddenly discovers that he/she cannot refuse the call to action.

William Johnston,
Silent Music

In order that prayer may become a dialogue of love, a unity of the human heart with God, we need to rest very much on the activity of the Holy Spirit. Mother Teresa of Calcutta once said that God is the friend of silence, and that silence is that which enables the touching of souls. In the silence of waiting and expectancy God speaks through us. In Mother Teresa and her sisters, in their work with starving, dying, abandoned men, women and children, we see examples of women in whom the false self has been burnt away by the love of Christ, and in whom contemplation and activity are completely united.

Mother Mary Clare,
Encountering the Depths

Ten thousand flowers in spring, the moon
    in autumn,
a cool breeze in summer, snow in winter.
If your mind isn't clouded by unnecessary

things,
this is the best season of your life.

Wu-Men (1183-1260),
taken from *The Enlightened Heart*

4
The Work of the Spirit

Abba Lot went to see Abba Joseph and said: Abba, as much as I am able I practice a small rule, a little fasting, some prayer and meditation, and remain quiet, and as much as possible I keep my thoughts clean. What else should I do? Then the old man stood up and stretched out his hands toward heaven, and his fingers became like ten torches of flame. And he said: If you wish, you can become all flame.

Yushi Nomura,
Sayings from the Desert Fathers

My soul thirsts for God,
the God of life,
when shall I go to see
the face of God?...

In the daytime may Yahweh
command his love to come,
and by night may his song be on my lips,
a prayer to the God of my life!

Psalm 42:1-2,8

Take care not to imagine that in this unison of the Word with the

44

soul we believe there to be some bodily element.... This union is in the spirit, because God is a Spirit.... The Spouse receives Him by a special gift in her inmost heart, coming down from heaven, and all at once possesses Him whom she desires, not under any definite form, but obscurely infused; not appearing clearly but making His presence felt; and doubtless all the more delightful in that His presence is secret, and does not appear outwardly.

This Word comes not sounding but penetrating; not speaking but acting on the soul; not beating upon the ear but blandishing the heart. This is a Face that has no form, but impresses a form upon the soul; not striking the eyes of the body but making glad the countenance of the heart.

St Bernard of Clairvaux (1090-1153),
Sermon of the Canticle

The Spirit too comes to help us in our weakness. For when we cannot choose words in order to pray properly, the Spirit himself expresses our plea in a way that could never be put into words, and God who knows everything in our hearts knows perfectly well what he means and that the pleas of the saints expressed by the Spirit are according to the mind of God.

Romans 8:26-7

With the mind right the individual self comes into flower. With the self in flower the family becomes an ordered harmony. With the families ordered harmoniously the state is efficiently   governed. With states efficiently governed, the Great Society is at peace.

Thus from the Son of Heaven down to the common people there is unity: in this, that for everybody the bringing of the individual self to flower is to be taken as the root. Since that is so, for the root to be out of order and the branches to be in order is an impossibility.

Confucius (551-479 BC),
taken from *The Analects of Confucius*

God's call is mysterious: it comes in the darkness of faith. It is so fine, so subtle, that it is only with the deepest silence within us that we can hear it.

And yet nothing is so decisive and overpowering for a person on this earth, nothing surer or stronger.

This call is uninterrupted: God is always calling us! But there are distinctive moments in this call of his, moments which leave a permanent mark on us — moments which we never forget.

Carlo Carretto (1910-89),
Letters from the Desert

It is the heart that experiences God, not the reason.

Blaise Pascal (1623-62),
Pensées

Listen for the voice of the Spirit,
for that which enlarges the mind,
frees the heart, brings together
what was scattered and lost,
holds fast in unswerving fidelity,
instills peace, renews confidence,
comforts and endures. Happy are
you if you hear that voice!

Carrin Dunne,
Behold Woman

An aged Brahman came to the Buddha bearing gifts in either hand, and eager to receive enlightenment. Said the Blessed One: 'Drop it.' The Brahman let fall one of his gifts. Again the order came: 'Drop it.' The Brahman let fall the other gift and remained empty-handed. 'Drop it,' came the order yet again. The Brahman was for the moment at a loss, then smiled, for he had attained enlightenment.

Zen Buddhist story

On this mountain he will remove
the mourning veil covering all peoples,

and the shroud enwrapping all nations,
he will destroy Death for ever.
The Lord your God will wipe away
the tears from every cheek;
he will take away his people's shame
everywhere on earth,
for he has said so.
That day it will be said: See, this is our God
in whom we hoped for salvation;
Our God is the one in whom we hoped.
We exult and we rejoice
that he has saved us;
for the hand of the Lord
rests on this mountain.

Isaiah 25: 7-10

We die on the day when our lives cease to be illumined by the steady radiance renewed daily, of a wonder, the source of which is beyond reason.

Dag Hammerskjöld (1905-61),
Markings

And it is with this belief and this knowledge
    that I say,
You are not enclosed within your bodies, nor
    confined to house or fields.
That which is you dwells above the mountain and
    roves with the wind.
It is not a thing that crawls into the sun for
    warmth or digs holes into darkness for safety,
But a thing free, a spirit that envelops the
    earth and moves in the ether...
But you do not see, nor do you hear, and it is well.
The veil that clouds your eyes shall be lifted
    by the hands that wove it.
And the clay that fills your ears shall be
    pierced by those fingers that kneaded it.
And you shall see

And you shall hear.
Yet you shall not deplore having known blindness
    nor regret having been deaf.
For in that day you shall know the hidden purposes
    in all things,
And you shall bless darkness as you would
    bless light.

Kahlil Gibran (1883-1931),
The Prophet

The wonderful beauty of prayer is that the opening our heart is as natural as the opening of a flower. Just as to let a flower open and bloom it is only necessary to let it be, so if we simply are, if we become and remain still and silent, our heart cannot but be open: the Spirit cannot but pour through into our whole being. It is this we have been created for.

Dom John Main (1926-82),
Community of Love

Set me as a seal on your heart,
Like a seal on your arm.
For love is strong as death,
Passionate love as relentless as death.
The flash of it is a flash of fire.
A flame of God himself.
Love no flood can quench, nor torrent drown.

Song of Songs 8:6-7

Drink the water from your own wells
Fresh water from your own source.

Proverbs 5:15

Men are continually seeking retreats for themselves, in the country or by the sea or among the hills. And thou, thyself, art wont to yearn after the like. Yet all this is the surest folly, for it is open to thee, every hour, to retire into thyself. And where can man find a calmer, more restful haven than in his own soul? Most of all, he whose inner state is so ordered that he has only to penetrate thither to find himself in the midst of a great peace — the peace that, to my mind, is synonymous with orderliness. Therefore, betake thee freely to this city of refuge, there to be made new.

Marcus Aurelius Antoninus (AD 121-80)

Don't strain after more light than you've got yet: just wait quietly. God holds you when you cannot hold Him, and when the time comes to jump He will see to it that you do jump — and you will find you are not frightened then. But probably all that is a long way ahead still. So just be supple in His hands and let Him mould you (as He is doing) for His own purposes, responding with very simple acts of trust and love.

Evelyn Underhill (1875-1941),
The Letters of Evelyn Underhill

When the Spirit has come to reside in someone, that person cannot stop praying; for the Spirit prays without ceasing in him. No matter if he is asleep or awake, prayer is going on in his heart all the time. He may be eating or drinking, he may be resting or working — the incense of prayer will ascend spontaneously from his heart....His thoughts will be prompted by God. The slightest stirring of his heart is like a voice which sings in silence and in secret to the Invisible.

St Isaac of Syria (sixth century),
Teach us to Pray

Then I am going to take you from among the nations and gather you together from all the foreign countries, and bring you home to your own land. I shall pour clean water over you and you will be cleansed; I shall cleanse you of all your defilement and all your idols. I shall give you a new heart, and put a new spirit in you; I shall remove the heart of stone from your bodies and give you a heart of flesh instead. I shall put my spirit in you, and make you keep my laws and sincerely respect my observances. You will live in the land which I gave your ancestors. You shall be my people and I will be your God.

Ezekiel 36:24-8

O God, do not let me take away from you the time that belongs
to you in contemplation.

Thomas Merton (1915-68),
The Sign of Jonas

I look not at the tongue and speech, I look
   at the spirit and the inward feeling
I look into the heart to see whether it be lowly,
   though the words uttered be not lowly.
Enough of phrases and conceits and metaphors! I
   want burning, burning, burning: become familiar with that
   burning!
Light up a fire of love in thy soul, burn all
   thought and expression away!
O Moses, they that know the conventions are of
   one sort,
they whose souls burn are of another.
The religion of Love is apart from all religions.
The Lovers of God have no religion but God alone.

Jalal ud-din Rumi (1207-73)

We and God have business with each other; and in opening our
selves to his influence our deepest destiny is fulfilled.

William James (1842-1910),
Varieties of Religious Experience

This call comes to college students, housewives, insurance sales-
men and prisoners. It comes to religious, diocesan priests, Prot-
estant clergy and rabbis. It comes to whom it comes. It is given
to whom it is given. We can ask for it with great desire (and to
do so is a sign that most likely it has already been given). But we
cannot make it happen. Like everything real, it simply comes to
us. It simply appears as an unexpected gift. And in appearing,

obscurely and secretly in the hidden recesses of our hearts, it awaits our response — our yes to the transforming union that is held out to us.

James Finley,
The Awakening Call

O where can I go from your spirit,
Or where can I flee from your face?
If I climb the heavens, you are there.
If I lie in the grave, you are there.
If I take the wings of the dawn
and dwell at the sea's further end,
even there your hand would lead me,
your right hand would hold me fast.
If I say: 'Let the darkness hide me
and the light around me be night,'
even darkness is not dark for you
and the night is as clear as the day.

Psalm 139:7-12

When the signs of age begin to mark my body (and still more when they touch my mind); when the ill that is to diminish me or carry me off strikes from without or is born within me; when the painful moment comes in which I suddenly awaken to the fact that I am ill or growing old; and above all at the last moment when I feel I am losing hold of myself and am absolutely passive in the hands of the great unknown forces that have formed me; in all those dark moments, O God, grant that I may understand that it is you (provided only my faith is strong enough) who are painfully parting the fibres of my being in order to penetrate to the very marrow of my substance and bear me away within yourself.

Pierre Teilhard de Chardin (1881-1955),
The Divine Milieu

A person is deemed worthy of constant prayer once he has become a dwelling-place of the Spirit. For unless someone has received the gift of the Comforter, in all certainty he will not be able to accomplish this constant prayer in quiet. But once the Spirit dwells in someone, as the Apostle says, the Spirit never ceases but prays continuously: then whether he sleeps or wakes, prayer is never absent from that person's soul.

If he eats or drinks, goes to sleep or is active; yes, even if he is sunk in deep sleep, the sweet fragrance of prayer effortlessly breathes in his heart. Then he is in the possession of prayer that knows no limit. For at all times, even when he is outwardly still, prayer constantly ministers within him secretly.

The silence of the serene is prayer, as one of those clothed in Christ says, for their thoughts are divine stirrings. The stirring of a pure mind constitutes still utterances, by means of which such people sing in a hidden way to the hidden God.

St Isaac of Syria (sixth century),
taken from *The Joy of the Saints*

Unless a wheat grain falls to the ground and dies,
it remains a single grain;
but if it dies
it yields a rich harvest.

John 12:24

This is one of the most important effects of meditation, that you begin to find a guidance in your life: that you are guided to meet the right people, to go to the right place, to do the right thing, and you begin to see that you are not managing your life just by yourself. God himself is acting in you. It is a very specific grace of meditation when you get that sense of guidance in your life, a visible sign; it is akin to what Jung called synchronicity.

Bede Griffiths (1907-93),
The New Creation in Christ

'The Holy Spirit will come upon you' the angel answered 'and the power of the Most High will cover you with its shadow. And so the child will be holy and will be called Son of God'....

'I am the handmaid of the Lord,' said Mary 'let what you have said be done unto me.'

Luke 1:35, 38

To contemplate is to move beyond your own activity and become activated by the inner power of the Holy Spirit. It means to be swept up into the threefold love current of Father, Son and Holy Spirit. In the silent prayer of the heart, a gift of the Spirit praying within you, you move beyond feelings, emotions, even thoughts. The Spirit is so powerfully operative that imagining or reasoning can only be noise that disturbs the silent communication of God at the core of your being.

If you introduce 'noise' by speaking words and fashioning images of God, then you are limiting his freedom to speak his word as he wishes, when he wishes. The Holy Spirit frees you so God can give himself to you. With utter freedom and joy, respond always in deep silence and humble self-surrender to his inner presence.

George A. Maloney,
Alone with the Alone

Christmas is the feast
of the divine
explosion,
the
love
of
God
revealed
in the poverty of Christ.

Dom John Main (1926-82)

Earth is crammed with Heaven
and every common bush
on fire with God.
But only he who sees
takes off his shoes.
The rest sit around

and pluck blackberries.

Elizabeth Barrett Browning (1806-61),
Browning Poetical Works

The commitment of lay people and those in active ministries to contemplation is a new way of following Christ in our time. Just as the Spirit created a new way of following Christ at the close of the age of martyrdom by inspiring Anthony with his vision of the monastic lifestyle, so now the Holy Spirit is inviting lay persons and those in active ministries to become contemplatives where they are: to move beyond the restricted world of selfishness into service of their communities, and to join all others of goodwill in addressing the global problems of our time: poverty, hunger, oppression, violence, and above all, the refusal to love.

Thomas Keating,
Invitation to Love

O Lord, I cried to you for help
and you, my God, have healed me.
To you, Lord, I cried, to my God
I made my appeal.
The Lord listened and had pity.
The Lord came to my help.
For me you have changed my mourning into dancing.
You have removed my sackcloth and girded me with joy.
So my soul sings psalms to you unceasingly.
O Lord my God, I will thank you for ever.

Psalm 29/30:3,9,11-12

God not only speaks his Word in silence from all eternity without any interruption, but he also hears this Word in perfect silence as an echo of his own reflected beauty and love. Through the silent gasp of love that is the Holy Spirit bringing God the Father together with his son, the heavenly Father hears his Word continually coming back to him in a perfect, eternal 'yes' of total, surrendering love that is again the Holy Spirit.

George Maloney,
Alone with the Alone

For anyone who is in Christ there is a new creation; the old creation has gone, and now the new one is here.

2 Corinthians 5:17

What is born of the flesh is flesh;
what is born of the Spirit is spirit.
Do not be surprised when I say:
You must be born from above.
The wind blows wherever it pleases;
you hear its sound,
but you cannot tell where it comes from or
    where it is going.
That is how it is with all those who are born
    of the Spirit.

John 3:6-8

This experience of Christ is the Spirit suddenly swooping down on the believer as recounted in the Acts. It is the deep conviction through shock in the inmost recess of being that Christ is there, living and present, that His life and my life are an indivisible, twinned system of stars; that He is in the inmost recess of my life and I am in the inmost recess of His.

Henri le Saux/Abhishiktananda (1910-73),
The Eyes of Light

Someday, after mastering the winds, the waves, the tides and gravity, we shall harness for God the energies of love, and then, for the second time in the history of the world, man will discover fire.

Pierre Teilhard de Chardin (1881-1955),
Toward the Future

As for me, brethren, when I came to you I declared God's hidden secret without display of fine words or wisdom. I came before you weak as I was then and the world I spoke and the Gospel I proclaimed did not sway you with subtle arguments. It carried conviction by spiritual power so that your faith might be built not upon human wisdom but upon the power of God.

1 Corinthians 2:4-5

5
Be Still

Without going outside, you may know the
    whole world.
Without looking through the window, you
    may see the ways of heaven.
The farther you go, the less you know.

Thus the sage knows without travelling;
He sees without looking;
He works without doing.

Lao Tzu (570-490 BC),
Tao Te Ching

The genuine Christian tradition, taught uninterruptedly for the
first fifteen centuries, is that contemplation is the normal evolution
of a genuine spiritual life and hence open to all Christians.

This tradition is summed up by Gregory the Great at the end
of the sixth century. He described contemplation as a knowledge
of God that is impregnated with love. For Gregory, contemplation
is the fruit of reflection on the Word of God in Scripture and at
the same time a gift of God. It is a resting in God. In this resting
or stillness the mind and heart are not actively seeking Him, but
are beginning to experience — taste — what they have been
seeking. This places them in a state of repose, tranquillity, and

profound interior peace. It is not the suspension of all action, but a mingling of a very simplified thought and the loving experience of God.

Thomas Keating,
Finding Grace at the Centre

Unless there is a still center
in the middle of the storm
Unless a person in the midst of all their activities
preserves a secret room in their heart where they stand
alone before God, unless we do this we will lose all sense
of spiritual direction and be torn to pieces.

Anonymous fourth-century desert monk

Contemplation is a country whose center is everywhere and whose circumference is nowhere. You do not find it by travelling but by standing still.

Thomas Merton (1915-68),
Seeds of Contemplation

Oh Lord, my heart is not lifted up,
    my eyes are not raised too high;
I do not occupy myself with things
    too great and too marvelous for me.
But I have calmed and quieted my soul,
    like a child that is quieted is my soul.
O Israel, hope in the Lord
    from this time forth and for evermore.

Psalm 131:2-3

Inner stillness is necessary if we are to be in perfect control of our faculties and if we are to hear the voice of the Spirit speaking to us.

There can be no stillness without discipline, and the discipline of external silence can help us towards that inner tranquillity which is at the heart of authentic religious experience.

In meditation we take steps to achieve this stillness. We quieten our bodies and our emotions, then gradually allow the mind to become single-pointed.

Stillness within one individual can affect society beyond measure.

Bede Griffiths (1907-93),
The Universal Christ

The greatest revelation is stillness.

Lao Tzu (570-490 BC),
Tao Te Ching

When there is a complete silence of the whole being, or a stillness unaffected by surface movements, then we can become aware of a Self, a spiritual substance of our being, an existence exceeding even the soul's individuality, spreading itself into universality, surpassing all dependence on any natural form of action, extending itself upwards into a transcendence of which the limits are not visible. It is these liberations of the spiritual path in us which are the spiritual evolution in nature.

Sri Aurobindo (1872-1950),
The Evolution of Spiritual Man

Tokusan was studying Zen under Ryutan.
One night Tokusan came to Ryutan
and asked many questions.

The Teacher said,
'The night is getting old —
why don't you retire?'

So Tokusan bowed,
and as he opened the screen to get out
he observed,
'It is very dark outside.'

Ryutan offered Tokusan a lighted candle

to find his way,
but first as Tokusan received it,
Ryutan blew it out.

At that moment
the mind of Tokusan was opened.

A Zen koan

But this stillness before the Word will exert its influence upon the whole day. If we have learned to be silent before the Word, we shall also learn to manage our silence and our speech during the day.
　　The silence of the Christian is listening silence, humble stillness, that may be interrupted any time for the sake of humility.

Dietrich Bonhoeffer (1906-45),
Modern Spirituality Series

I laugh when I hear that the fish in the water is thirsty.

Perceivest thou not how the god is in thine own house, that thou wanderest from forest to forest so listlessly?

In thy home is the Truth. Go where thou wilt, to Benares or to Mathura; if thy soul is a stranger to thee, the whole world is unhomely.

Kabir (1440-1518),
taken from One Hundred Poems of Kabir

For thus saith the Lord God, the Holy One of Israel: in waiting and rest shall you be saved: in quietness and confidence shall be your strength.

Isaiah 30:15

There is no need to run outside for better seeing. Nor to peer from a window. Rather abide at the center of your being; For the more you leave it, the less you learn. Search your heart and see if he is wise who takes each turn; The way to do is to be.

Lao Tzu (570-490 BC)
The Way of Life According to Lao Tzu

Let us, then, labor for an inward stillness —
An inward stillness and an inward healing;
That perfect silence where the lips and heart
Are still, and we no longer entertain
Our own imperfect thoughts and vain opinions,
But God alone speaks in us, and we wait
In singleness of heart, that we may know
His will, and in silence of our spirits,
That we may do His will and do that only.

Henry Wadsworth Longfellow (1807-82),
Favourite Poems

'You must come away to some lonely place all by yourselves and rest awhile'; for there were so many coming and going that the apostles had no time even to eat. So they went off in a boat to a lonely place where they could be by themselves.

Mark 6:31

At the still point of the turning world. Neither
    flesh nor fleshless;
Neither from nor towards; at the still point,
    there the dance is,
But neither arrest nor movement, And do not call
    it fixity,
Where past and future are gathered. Neither
    movement from nor towards,
Neither ascent nor decline. Except for the point,
    the still point,
There would be no dance, and there is only the
    dance.

I can only say, *there* we have been: but I cannot
  say where.
And I cannot say, how long, for that is to place
  it in time.

T.S. Eliot (1888-1965),
Four Quartets

Make peace with yourself and heaven and earth will make peace
with you. Endeavour to enter your own inner cell, and you will
see the heavens, because the one and the other are one and the
same, and when you enter one you see the two.

St Isaac of Syria (sixth century),
taken from *The Joy of the Saints*

Make your heart empty
Waiting in stillness.
Banish your busy thoughts
Out from your mind;
Return to quiet.
Take into your calmness
The presence of God,
Overflowing with love,
Stilling all fear,
Safeguard from all danger;
Rest in God's Peacefulness.

Lao Tzu (570-490 BC),
Tao Te Ching

I said to my soul, be still and wait without hope
For hope would be hope for the wrong things; wait without love
For love would be love of the wrong thing; there is yet faith
But the faith and the love and the hope are all in the waiting.
Wait without thought, for you are not ready for thought:
so the darkness shall be the light, and the stillness the dancing.

T.S. Eliot (1888-1965),
Four Quartets

Prayer of the heart is not a technique or even a certain stage in the total process of growth in prayer. The hesychastic Fathers constantly describe it as forcing the mind down into the heart. It is basically an affective attitude that seeks to transcend the limitations of human words and mental images to reach an inner 'still point' where God and man meet in silent self-surrender.

George Maloney,
Prayer of the Heart

A mind that is fast is sick.
A mind that is slow is sound.
A mind that is still is divine.

Meher Baba (1894-1969)
(Meher Baba Info)

The very best and utmost of attainment in this life is to remain still and let God act and speak in thee.

Meister Eckhart (1260-1327),
Sermons and Treatises

Rest in the Lord; wait patiently for Him....be silent to God and let Him mould thee. Keep still, and He will mould thee to the right shape.

Martin Luther (1483-1546)

Look well, O soul, upon thyself
    lest spiritual ambition
    should mislead and blind thee
    to thy essential task:
        to wait in quietness,
        to knock and persevere in humble faith.

Gilbert Shaw,
The Face of God

I do my utmost to attain emptiness;
I hold firmly to stillness.
The myriad creatures all rise together
And I watch their return.
The teeming creatures
All return to their separate roots.
Returning to one's roots is known as stillness.

Lao Tzu (570-490 BC),
Tao Te Ching

The answer was always quietly there, only our questions drowned it out.

David Steindl-Rast,
A Listening Heart

Still water is like glass.
Look in it and you will see the bristles on your chin.
It is a perfect level
so that carpenters can use it.
If water is so clear, so level,
how much more the human mind?
The heart of a wise person is tranquil.
It is the mirror of heaven and earth
reflecting everything.

Emptiness, stillness, tranquillity,
reserve, silence, non-action;
these mirror heaven and earth.
This is perfect Tao.
Wise people find here their point of rest.

Chuang Tzu (369-286 BC),
The Way of Chuang Tzu

God is a tranquil Being, and abides in a tranquil eternity. So must thy spirit become a tranquil and clear little pool, wherein the serene light of God can be mirrored.

Gerhard Terteegen (1697-1769)

All the troubles of life come upon us because we refuse to sit quietly for a while each day in our rooms.

Blaise Pascal (1623-62),
Pensées

Empty yourself of everything
Let the mind rest in peace.
The ten thousand things rise and fall while
the Self watches their return.
They grow and flourish and then return to
the source.
Returning to the source is stillness, which
is the way of nature.
The way of nature is unchanging.
Knowing constancy is insight.
Not knowing constancy leads to disaster.
Knowing constancy, the mind is open.
With an open mind, you will be openhearted.
Being openhearted, you will act royally.
Being royal, you will attain the divine.
Being divine, you will be at one with the Tao.
Being at one with the Tao is eternal.
And though the body dies,
The Tao will never pass away.

Lao Tzu (570-490 BC),
Tao Te Ching

There is hardly ever a complete silence in our soul. God is whispering to us well-nigh incessantly. Whenever the sounds of the world die out in the soul, or sink low, then we hear these whisperings of God. He is always whispering to us, only we do not always hear, because of the noise, hurry, and distraction which life causes as it rushes on.

Frederick William Faber (1814-63)

Silence is the doorway into the need of the world, the condition of the prayer which arises out from the heart of the universe, because it expresses the love of Christ, crucified and risen for the world. Such profound prayer, however, is not concerned only with the world as a whole, but also with the most mundane details of our ordinary everyday lives. Prayer is not a part-time occupation, and there can no more be part-time contemplatives than part-time Christians. Without the contemplative dimension in our lives, we cannot be fully human. This contemplative dimension is the fruit of our willingness to meet the discipline of learning to wait in silence and stillness, as well as the boredom and loneliness and sometimes the apparent emptiness which confront us in the waiting. Contemplation and action are both necessary to basic stability. There is a need to take regular times of quiet in order to be disciplined in the generous giving of self in our activity.

Mother Mary Clare,
Encountering the Depths

If you seek contemplation, Merton would tell you, you will probably never find it; but if you dare open your heart to your own inner truth and to God's grace, contemplation may enter your life unobserved. Then, perhaps for the first time, you will know who you are and in knowing yourself you will know God; for it is He, Merton would say, who holds within Himself the secret of your own identity.

William H. Shannon
Thomas Merton's Dark Path

6
Meditation and the One Little Word

We call the prayer-word 'mantra.' This is a Sanskrit term for what Cassian calls a 'formula' of prayer and the *Cloud*, 'one little word.' The term 'mantra' has now entered English usage, just as the Hebrew 'amen' or the Greek 'Christos.' Perhaps this is a sign of the vast and mysterious process by which East and West are being married today. But there is no special significance in its being an Eastern term. The advantage of using it is precisely that it does make us realize that this *meditation* is different from what we may think prayer to be. It is not about talking to God or thinking about God or asking for anything. The word 'maranatha' is Aramaic — Jesus' language — for 'Come, Lord.' It is one of the earliest recorded Christian prayers and was early used as what we would now call a mantra.

Laurence Freeman,
Light Within

Many so-called enlightened people regard this frequent repetition of a prayer phrase as useless and even trifling, calling it mechanical and a thoughtless occupation of simple people. But unfortunately they do not know how this repetition of the prayer phrase imperceptibly becomes rooted in the heart, sinks down into the inner life, becomes a delight, becomes, as it were, natural to the

soul, bringing it light and nourishment and leading it on to union
with God.

R.M. French (1884-1969)
The Way of a Pilgrim

We must acquire the habit of always being in communion with
God, without any image, any process of reasoning, any percepti-
ble movement of thought. Such is the true expression of prayer.
The essence of inner prayer, or standing before God with the mind
in the heart, consists precisely in this.

Bishop Theophane the Recluse (1815-94),
The Art of Prayer: An Orthodox Anthology

The invocation of the Name, rightly practised, involves us more
deeply in our appointed tasks, making us more efficient in our
actions, not cutting us off from others but linking us to them,
rendering us sensitive to their fears and anxieties in a way that we
never were before. The Jesus Prayer makes each of us into a
'person for others,' a living instrument of God's peace, a dynamic
center of reconciliation.

Kallistos Ware

We should endeavour to maintain
our minds in silence,
remote even from such thoughts
as may seem legitimate.
Let us constantly look into the depths
of our heart saying
Lord Jesus Christ, Son of God,
have mercy on me.
Recite the prayer attentively in this manner,
standing, sitting or reclining,
Enclose your mind in your heart...call upon God
with fervent desire,

in patient expectation,
turning away all thoughts.

John Cassian (AD 360-434),
The Classics of Western Spirituality

And so, having collected your mind within you, lead it into the channel of breathing through which air reaches the heart and, together with the inhaled air, force your mind to descend into the heart and remain there....When you thus enter into the place of the heart, as I have shown you...keep always to this doing, and it will teach you things which in no other way will you ever learn. Moreover, you should know that when your mind becomes firmly established in the heart, it must not remain there silent and idle, but it should constantly repeat the prayer: Lord Jesus Christ, Son of God, have mercy on me, and never cease.

St Nicephorus (758-828),
Writings from the Philokalia

Our mind will come to that pure prayer....This prayer is not occupied with the consideration of any image; moreover, it does not express itself by utterances or words; but with the purpose of the mind all on fire, the prayer is produced by an ineffable transport of the heart, by some insatiable keenness of spirit; and the mind being placed beyond all sense and visible matters, pours it forth to God with groanings and sighs that cannot be uttered.

Abba Isaac (fourth century),
The Classics of Western Spirituality

Practice intensely the mystical contemplations;
Leave behind the sense and the intellectual activities,
and all sensible and intelligible things;
Raise yourself to union in ignorance, with Him who is
above all being and all knowledge.

Dionysius the Areopagite (fifth/sixth century),
*Dionysius the Areopagite on the Divine Names
and the Mystical Theology*

69

8 June [1941], Sunday morning, 9.30. I think that I'll do it anyway; I'll 'turn inwards' for half an hour each morning before work, and listen to my inner voice. Lose myself. You could also call it meditation. I am still a bit wary of that word. But anyway, why not? A quiet half-hour within yourself. It's not enough just to move your arms and legs and all the other muscles about in the bathroom each morning. Man is body and spirit. And half an hour of exercises combined with half an hour of meditation can set the tone for the whole day.

But it's not so simple, that sort of 'quiet hour.' It has to be learnt. A lot of unimportant inner litter and bits and pieces have to be swept out first. Even a small head can be piled high inside with irrelevant distractions. True, there may be edifying emotions and thoughts, too, but the clutter is ever present. So let this be the aim of meditation: to turn one's innermost being into a vast empty plain, with none of that treacherous undergrowth to impede the view. So that something of 'God' can enter you, and something of 'Love' too.

Etty Hillesum (1914-43),
An Interrupted Life

In meditation I heard the Lord say, 'Which seems to you the better prayer, to pray to me with your heart or with your thoughts?'

'When you pray with your thoughts you know what you ask me and you understand what I say to you. When you sit still and give your heart to meditation, then you will receive thoughts that God has put into your mind.'

'I accept all your prayers whether you speak them, think in your heart, read, or listen to reading.'

'Fasting, penance and saying the daily offices are good when you are learning to pray, and I accept any form of prayer gladly, but you are much closer to me when you sit quietly in contemplation.'

Margery Kempe (1373-1439),
taken from *The Joy of the Saints*

When the nun Chiyono studied Zen under Bukko of Engaku she was unable to attain the fruits of meditation for a long time.

At last one moonlit night she was carrying water in an old pail bound with bamboo. The bamboo broke and the bottom fell out of the pail, and at that moment Chiyono was set free!

In commemoration, she wrote a poem:

> In this way and that I tried to save the
>   old pail
> Since the bamboo strip was weakening and
>   about to break
> Until at last the bottom fell out
> No more water in the pail!
> No more moon in the water!

Zen story
'No water, no moon'

Meditation is…a state of inner absorption in which the mind of the meditator flows continuously and spontaneously toward the object of meditation.

Swami Adeswarananda

An old man said: Constant prayer quickly straightens out our thoughts.

Yushi Nomura,
Sayings from the Desert Fathers

John Main proposes the word 'Maranatha' as a mantra. This means 'Come, Lord' and is undoubtedly one of the very oldest Christian prayers. St Paul uses it in his letter to the Corinthians, and St John uses it in his Revelation. When Paul wrote to the people of Corinth only twenty years after the death and resurrection of Jesus, he left the word in the original Aramaic language while he wrote the rest of the letter in Greek. There was no need to translate.

He knew that all the Christians who heard his letter would know what Maranatha meant. It is also believed that for the first generations of Christians it was a sort of password, a greeting meaningful only for the believer. And, not only is Maranatha a scriptural mantra, it also appears in the oldest fragment of the Eucharist that exists. Here in the invitation to receive communion the priest says:

> Praise to the Son of David.
> If anyone is holy, let him come.
> If anyone is not holy, let him repent.
> Maranatha. Amen.
> Come Lord.

> Certainly 'Maranatha,' 'Come Lord, come Lord Jesus,' is an invocation filled with love, confidence and longing.

Philippa Craig,
Living from Within

You meditate not to experience the experience. You meditate to enter into the experience.

Dom John Main (1926-82),
Moment of Christ

But now you put a question to me asking: 'How shall I think about Him, and what is He?' And to this I can only answer you, 'I do not know.' With your question you have brought me into that same darkness and into that same cloud of unknowing into which I would wish you to be in yourself. Through grace a man can have great knowledge of all other creatures and their works, and even the works of God Himself, and he can think of them all; but of God Himself no man can think. I would therefore leave all those things of which I can think and choose for my love that thing of which I cannot think.

And why is this so? He may well be loved, but He may not be thought of. He may be reached and held close by means of love, but by means of thought, never. And therefore even though it is good occasionally to think of the kindness and the great worth of God in particular aspects, and even though it is a joy that is a proper part of contemplation, nevertheless in this work it should be cast down and covered with a cloud of forgetting.

Anon (fourteenth century),
The Cloud of Unknowing

Meditation consists in learning to focus and to control the mind. When the mind is stilled, then the light of the intellect begins to shine. The mind is ordinarily scattered and dissipated, but gather the mind into one and then the pure light shines in the mirror which is oneself.

Speech is the movement by which we go out of ourselves to communicate to another. Meditation takes us within ourselves. It is a process of inner withdrawal, a centering in the place of inner detachment, a staying of the mind upon God.

Bede Griffiths (1907-93),
The Universal Christ

Contemplation is nothing else but a secret, peaceful, and loving infusion of God, which, if admitted, will set the soul on fire with the Spirit of Love.

St John of the Cross (1542-91),
Collected Works of St John of the Cross

As far as is possible, raise thyself up in knowing even unto union with Him Who is beyond all essence and all knowledge. For it is indeed by going out of thyself and out of all things with an irresistible leap, free and pure, that thou shalt raise thyself up to the pure and superessential ray of the divine darkness, after having abandoned all things and having liberated thyself from them all.

Then, delivered from all objects and from the very organs of contemplation (the contemplative) penetrates into the truly mystical Cloud of Unknowing in which he closes his eyes to all objects and knowledge and finds himself in utter intangibility and invisibility. He now belongs entirely to Him Who is beyond all, and belongs no longer to any thing, neither to himself, nor to any other being, and is thus united in the most noble union with Him Who is utterly unknowable, by the cessation of all knowledge in this

73

total unknowing he now knows with a knowledge that is beyond understanding.

Dionysius the Areopagite (sixth century),
Dictionnaire de Spiritualité

Thus ceaseless prayer keeps our mental air free from the dark clouds and winds of the spirits of evil. And when the air of the heart is pure, there is nothing to prevent the Divine light of Jesus shining in it.

Hesychius (fifth century),
*Writings from the Philokalia on Prayer
of the Heart*

He prays best who does not know he is praying.

St Anthony of Egypt (AD 251-350),
The Letters of St Anthony the Great

Christian meditation urges the repetition of a mantra for the full meditation time of thirty minutes. The repetition of a mantra is an act of concentration that focuses our attention. It is a way of turning from our egos and is therefore a way of silencing all thought and imagination for the whole prayer period. The concentration we bring to the act of repeating our mantra acts like a searchlight that directs its beam away from the self to the word being said. Its practice enables a letting go of, or disconnecting from, egocentricity.

In insisting that the mantra be repeated throughout the allotted prayer time, the tradition of Christian meditation provides a discipline that readies the heart for the complete turning toward the Divine Other, a turning free of ego-centeredness. This practice of dying to the ego does not diminish or divest us of all the gifts and goodness that makes us truly human; rather this practice puts us in direct contact with the reality of our humanness — the true self.

Eileen O'Hea,
Woman: Her Intuition for Otherness

The way we set out on this pilgrimage of 'other-centeredness' is to recite a short phrase, a word that is commonly called today a mantra. The mantra is simply a means of turning our attention beyond ourselves — a way of unhooking us from our own thoughts and concerns. Reciting the mantra brings us to stillness and to peace. We recite it for as long as we need to before we are caught up into the one prayer of Jesus. The general rule is that we must first learn to say it for the entire period of our meditation each morning and each evening and then to allow it to do its work of calming over a period of years.

Dom John Main (1926-82),
Moment of Christ

If you have never had any distractions you don't know how to pray.

Thomas Merton (1915-68),
Seeds of Contemplation

It is only in the awakening of the contemplative spirit, of a transcendent consciousness, that we come to this vision of unity. The method of realizing this vision has been close at hand in the way of mediation taught by Father John Main. I really feel that he made a breakthrough that has opened the way for Christians to go beyond the world of the senses and of concepts to the divine mystery itself and to allow that mystery to penetrate our lives and transform them.

It is a simple method, and yet it is so radical and fundamental that it really can change the world. This method of meditation, together with others, is spreading throughout the world. We must not isolate the Christian practice from others, because all are in search of the transcendent reality, whether they be Hindu, Buddhist, Muslim, Jewish or some other. All serious meditation is trying to go beyond the world of the senses and the mind, to open oneself to the divine mystery. You cannot name it, you cannot express it, you can only point towards it. In meditation, something in you opens up and the divine discloses itself. You cannot force it. You have to let go and allow it to reveal itself.

Bede Griffiths (1907-93),
The New Creation in Christ

This is the verse (the mantra) that the mind should unceasingly cling to until, strengthened by saying it over and over again and repeating it continually, it renounces and lets go of all the abundant riches of thought. Restricting itself to the poverty of this single verse it will come most easily to that first of the gospel beatitudes: for he says 'Blessed are the poor in spirit for theirs is the kingdom of heaven.'

John Cassian (AD 360-434),
The Classics of Western Spirituality

Choose one word or a little phrase which will express your love for him; and then go on repeating it in peace, without trying to form thoughts, motionless in love before God who is love.

Carlo Carretto (1910-89),
Letters from the Desert

The day will come when the mantra ceases to sound and we are lost in the eternal silence of God. The rule when this happens is not to try to possess this silence, to use it for one's own satisfaction. The clear rule is that as soon as we consciously realize that we are in this state of profound silence and begin to reflect about it we must gently and quietly return to our mantra.

Dom John Main (1926-82),
Moment of Christ

Those two times of daily meditation a day become times of spiritual work and times of powerful recreation. As times of renewal and refreshment the effects of those short periods of desirelessness overflow into daily life. You are not merely re-charging your batteries; you are making contact with an inexhaustible source of energy, the energy of divine being.

As we make contact with it, it flows into every corner of life with all its unlimited power. The contact with the ground of being is why those two simple and ordinary half-hours of meditation each day have such a transforming effect upon our lives. As they are times of being, not for wanting, do not even want any spiritual experience. Do not want anything to happen. Do not want God. Do not want the Spirit. Do not want to want.

Laurence Freeman,
The Selfless Self

Is it possible that in fidelity to silent waiting everything I could ever hope to receive from God, and infinitely more, lies waiting for me? Is it possible the nakedness and poverty of wordless prayer is my way, my discipleship to the risen Lord? Is it here in this silence that the Spirit waits with unutterable groanings to place on my lips the words, 'I and the Father are one?'...Somehow, deep in your heart, you already know the answer. It is this conviction, rooted in experience, that will allow no true peace without fidelity to the inner way of contemplative prayer.

James Finley,
The Awakening Call

Contemplation unites us with God at a vertical level where we transcend ourselves, the world and all our problems, and experience oneness with God. It is at the same time a mode of action at the horizontal level by which we go out from the centre of peace in God to the whole world. The further we go vertically towards God the further we can go horizontally towards men.

Bede Griffiths (1907-93),
The Universal Christ

If it suits you, you can have this naked intent wrapped up and enfolded in one word. In that case, in order that you may have a better grasp on it, take a short word of one syllable. One syllable is better than two, and the shorter the word the more suited it is to accomplish the work of the spirit.

Such a word is the word 'God' or the word 'Love.' Choose

whichever you wish, or another if you prefer, but let it be of one syllable.

Fasten this word to your heart so that it never leaves you, come what may. This word is to be your shield and your spear, whether in peace or in war.

With this word you are to beat upon the cloud and the darkness above you. With it you are to smite down every manner of thought under the cloud of forgetting. So much so, that if any thought should press upon you to ask you what you would have, answer it with no other words but this one word.

And if you should be tempted to analyze this word, answer that you will have it whole and undeveloped. If you will but hold fast, be sure that the temptation will not last long.

Anon (fourteenth century),
The Cloud of Unknowing

Seek God not happiness — this is the fundamental rule of all meditation.

Dietrich Bonhoeffer (1906-45),
Life Together

Among all the gifts which meditation bestows, there is one which I find to be the golden thread or chain holding all those precious jewels together. It is called harmony. The slow but sure sense of being gathered into a harmonious entity, of having one's identity nowhere else but in the One in whom we live and move and have our being. Could there be any greater sanity? Meditation gathers together all the disparate parts of ourselves so that we no longer are scattered and separate. I find that more and more I am losing this once almost frenetic sense of having to keep running in order to achieve...what?

Now, with the discipline of meditation I am learning to be still, both in body and in mind. I am also learning to be more attentive to my body by doing things like yoga. Best of all, I am learning as I go about my daily tasks of work or play or prayer, that it is right and good to be here just now doing whatever it is I am supposed to be doing. In a word, attentiveness and being in the present moment. Learning to be. A growing sense of vocation, a vocation of having the liberty to be at One. Our vocation is to be harmonious.

Madeleine Thompson,
Christian Meditation by Those Who Practice It

Gradually the silence becomes longer and we are simply absorbed in the mystery of God. The important thing is to have the courage and generosity to return to the mantra as soon as we become self-conscious of the silence.

Dom John Main (1926-82),
Moment of Christ

Of the method of continual prayer — Wherefore in accordance with that system...we must give you also the form of this spiritual contemplation on which you may always fix your gaze with its utmost steadiness...and manage by the practice of it and by meditation to climb to a still loftier height....And so for keeping up continual recollection of God this pious formula is to be ever set before you: O God, make speed to save me: O Lord, make haste to help me!

Abba Isaac (fourth century),
taken from *The Power of Prayer*

A Zen Story

ROSHI Tell me, what about your Zen? What are you doing?

JOHNSTON I'm doing what you, I suppose, would call 'gedo' Zen.

ROSHI Very good! Very good! Many Christians do that. But what precisely do you mean by 'gedo Zen'?

JOHNSTON I mean that I am sitting silently in the presence of God without words or thoughts or images or ideas.

ROSHI Your God is everywhere?

JOHNSTON Yes.

ROSHI And you are wrapped around in God?

JOHNSTON Yes.

ROSHI And you experience this?

JOHNSTON Yes

ROSHI Very good! Very good! Just continue this way. Just keep on. And eventually you will find that God will disappear and only Johnston San will remain.

This remark shocked me....I said with a smile, 'God will not disappear. But Johnston might well disappear and only God will be left.'

'Yes, yes,' he answered smilingly. 'It's the same thing. That is what I mean.'

William Johnston,
Christian Zen

Time and again the practical advice of masters of prayer is summed up in the simple injunction: 'Say your mantra'; 'Use this little word.' The Cloud of Unknowing advises, 'and pray not in many words but in a little word of one syllable. Fix this word fast to your heart so that it is always there come what may. With this word you will suppress all thoughts.'

Abbot Chapman, in his famous letter of Michaelmas 1920 from Downside, describes the simple, faithful use of a mantra which he had discovered more from his own courageous perseverance in prayer than from teachers. He had rediscovered a simple enduring tradition of prayer that entered the West through Monasticism, and first entered Western Monasticism through John Cassian in the late fourth century. Cassian himself received it from the holy men of the desert who placed its origin back beyond living memory to Apostolic times.

The venerable tradition of the mantra in Christian prayer is above all attributable to its utter simplicity. It answers all the requirements of the master's advice on how to pray because it leads us to a harmonious, attentive stillness of mind, body and spirit. It requires no special talent or gift apart from serious intent and the courage to persevere. 'No one,' Cassian said, 'is kept away from purity of heart by not being able to read nor is rustic simplicity any obstacle to it for it lies close at hand for all if only they will by constant repetition of this phrase keep the mind and heart attentive to God.'

Our mantra is the ancient Aramaic prayer, 'Maranatha, Maranatha,' 'Come Lord. Come Lord Jesus.'

Dom John Main
Word Into Silence

You cannot do this prayer by will power. The more effort you put
into it, the less well it goes. When you catch yourself trying hard,
relax and let go. Introduce the sacred word gently, incredibly
gently, as if you were laying a feather on a piece of absorbent
cotton.

Of course, when thoughts are flying at you like baseballs, you
look around for some means to protect yourself. But swatting them
out of the park is not the way to do it. You should honestly say,
'Well, I am being pummeled with these thoughts,' and put up with
them, remembering that if you just wait, they will all pass by. Do
not oppose violence with violence. This prayer is totally nonvio-
lent.

Thomas Keating,
Open Mind, Open Heart

If a soul is seeking God, its Beloved is seeking it still more.

When the soul reflects that God is the guide of its blind self,
then the main preoccupation will be to see that it sets no obstacle
in the way of its guide, the Holy Spirit, upon the road by which
God is leading it.

The soul then has to walk with loving advertence to God,
without making specific acts, and exerting no effort on its own
part. It must keep a simple, pure and loving awareness, like one
who gazes with the awareness of love.

The soul must be attached to nothing, whether of sense or
spirit, which would introduce noise into the deep silence. There
the voice of God speaks to the heart in this secret place, in utmost
peace and tranquillity.

St John of the Cross (1542-91),
taken from *The Joy of the Saints*

This word will be your defence in conflict and peace. Use it to
beat upon the cloud of darkness above you and subdue all

81

distractions, consigning them to the Cloud of Forgetting beneath you. Should some thought go on annoying you, answer with this one word alone. Do this and I assure you these thoughts will vanish.

Anon (fourteenth century),
The Cloud of Unknowing

The way of meditation is essentially simple. There are no special theories, complicated techniques, no preconditioned dogma that you have to hold or subscribe to. It is essentially simple because it is experiential. It is, in fact, a discipline rather than a technique. We have to begin where we are, with whatever kind of faith we may have. All that you need to do is begin; once you have begun you realize that you are entering into a spiritual discipline and that the purpose of a discipline is to set you free.

The essence of meditation in this tradition is the discipline of saying your word. It is entering into a faith-filled silence of mind and body where we leave words and thoughts behind. We are not thinking about God, we are not thinking about ourselves, we are not thinking about relationships, we are not thinking about peace. We are not thinking or imagining any of these as ideas. We leave words and thoughts and 'God' behind. We sit still.

Laurence Freemen,
Short Span of Days

There is only one failure in meditation: the failure to meditate faithfully. A Hindu proverb says, 'Miss one morning, and you need seven to make it up.' or as Saint John of the Cross expressed it, 'He who interrupts the course of his spiritual exercises and prayer is like a man who allows a bird to escape from his hand; he can hardly catch it again.'

Eknath Easwaran,
Meditation

Now, for those of us committed to the pilgrimage of meditation, we must remember the utter ordinariness of meditation. We must return to it daily, every morning and every evening in simplicity of spirit, not with demands, expectations for extraordinary phenomena, but sitting down to meditate is what our spirit requires. It is this ordinariness that gives to our meditation the potential for that radical expansion of spirit beyond ourselves into God; that is why commitment to the simplicity of the practice is of such supreme importance.

When we sit down to meditate we leave all thought, all desires behind and are content to be in the Presence. If we want to live our lives to the full, each of us must find our way into this perfect equilibrium of the human and divine, not just in theory. Our own humanity must be brought into harmonious oneness with God, who dwells in our hearts. This mystery dwells within each one of us; our meditation is the outer expression of our commitment.

Once we begin to move towards this reality we begin to understand more and more clearly that the ordinary is shot through with the extraordinary.

Dom John Main (1926-82),
from a talk

Meditation achieves its purpose when it brings you to a point of bafflement and darkness, wherein you can no longer think of God or imagine Him and are consequently forced to reach out to Him by blind faith, and hope and love. When you reach this point you must not be discouraged by the seeming futility of meditation; instead, you should relax 'in a simple contemplative gaze that keeps your attention peacefully aware of Him hidden somewhere in this deep cloud,' into which you have entered.

William H. Shannon,
Thomas Merton's Dark Path

At this point my understanding of the word spirituality has greatly expanded, along with my consciousness. I believe it means the extent to which I can open my heart to allow the Holy Spirit to activate my life. I find that silence and solitude are becoming increasingly important, and I am aware of the presence of God, both within me and in the whole universe. I simply know that God is present and I know it with a deep certainty.

As this century progresses we are becoming increasingly aware that there is a way of knowing which is not transmitted by the senses; it is extrasensory or intuitive knowledge, directly communicated by the Holy Spirit. Meditation greatly enhances a human being's ability to know intuitively. Intuitive knowledge is often prophetic. Meditation is the human transforming element in our religion, indeed in all the world's great religions. Every religion has its contemplative dimension. Meditation is our common meeting ground. Contemplation is our great common denominator.

If the spiritual journey is considered as a gradual transformation, as a process of being psychologically undone and remade through our meditation, there have been times when I mentally rebelled. There have been periods of aridity, of boredom, a feeling that God was no longer present. However I could see my own motives clearly. Everything I did was tinged with pride. There was an overwhelming sense of my own sinfulness. Humility grew slowly. I had to learn to live with the feeling of helplessness and to trust God. There was a distinct feeling of loss of control. I had to learn to trust God in the darkness when He no longer seemed to be present. I had to say yes to God every day. Not my will but Yours! This letting go has developed through Christian meditation. It has changed my life. It *is* the transformation.

Jill Black,
Christian Meditation by those who Practice It

Repeating a mantra sounds so simple that most people cannot believe it works until they try it. For one thing, many consider it mere mechanical repetition — a job for any tape recorder. But I would say that a journey makes a better analogy. Each step on a journey superficially resembles the others, but each uniquely takes you into new territory and moves you closer to your destination. In just the same way, the repetitions of the mantra are superficially alike, but each takes you ever deeper into consciousness and closer to the goal of love and joyful awareness.

Eknath Easwaran,
Meditation

This leads us back to the discipline of letting go. The Sermon on the Mount is a challenge to let go of our anxieties, fears, moralistic religiosity and the like. Taking one gigantic step into the unknown we are challenged to let go of all spiritual attachments such as discursive thinking, images, concepts and symbols. We renounce what we know about God in our openness to what might be revealed to the reality of an experience that we no longer control. We must live in the *now* of God's Presence to what is, to our life and that of the entire cosmos.

We cannot afford to look into our past with anxiety, guilt or frustrated hopes. We let go of time and space, including spiritual space. The seeker of God clings to nothing; the seeker answers the call to the desert.

> François C. Gerard (1924-91),
> *Going on a Journey*

If you ask me just precisely how one is to go about doing the contemplative work of love, I am at a complete loss. All I can say is I pray that Almighty God in his great goodness and kindness will teach you himself. For in all honesty I must admit I do not know. And no wonder, for it is a divine activity and God will do it in whomever he chooses. No one can earn it.

Paradoxical as it may seem, it would not even occur to a person — no, nor to an angel or saint — to desire contemplative love were it not already alive within that person. I believe, too, often our Lord deliberately chooses to work in those who have been habitual sinners rather than in those who, by comparison, have never grieved him at all. Yes he seems to do this very often. for I think he wants us to realize that he is all-merciful and almighty, and that he is perfectly free to work as he pleases, where he pleases, and when he pleases.

> Anon (fourteenth century),
> *The Cloud of Unknowing*

Meditation is one of the ways in which the spiritual man keeps himself awake. It is not really a paradox that it is precisely in meditation that most aspirants for religious perfection grow dull and fall asleep. Meditative prayer is a stern discipline, and one which cannot be learned by violence. It requires unending courage and perseverance, and those who are not willing to work at it patiently will finally end in compromise. Here, as elsewhere, compromise is only another name for failure.

Thomas Merton (1915-68),
Thoughts in Solitude

Concentration *without effort* — that is to say where there is nothing to suppress and where contemplation becomes as natural as breathing and the beating of the heart — is the state of consciousness (i.e. thought, imagination, feeling and will) of perfect calm, accompanied by the complete relaxation of the nerves and the muscles of the body. It is the profound silence of desires, of preoccupations, of the imagination, of the memory and of discursive thought.

One may say that the entire being becomes like the surface of calm water, reflecting the immense presence of the starry sky and its indescribable harmony. And the waters are deep, they are so deep! And the silence grows, ever increasing...what silence! Its growth takes place through regular waves which pass, one after the other, through your being: one wave of silence followed by another wave of more profound silence....Have you ever drunk silence? If in the affirmative, you know what concentration without effort is.

To begin with there are moments, subsequently minutes, then 'quarters of an hour' for which complete silence or 'concentration without effort' lasts. With time, the silence of concentration without effort becomes a fundamental element always present in the life of the soul. It is like the perpetual service at the church of Sacre Coeur de Montmartre which takes place, whilst in Paris one works, one trades, one amuses oneself, one sleeps, one dies....It is in like manner that a 'perpetual service' of silence is established in the soul, which continues all the same when one is active, when one works, or when one converses. This 'zone of silence' being once established, you can draw from it both for rest and for work. Then you will have not only concentration without effort, but also activity without effort.

Anonymous spiritual writer,
Meditations on the Tarot

If we believe in a God who is always with us, then everything we do is known. Of all possible encounters, prayer and especially meditation, requires no façade. It will do no good to worry about putting our best foot forward, literally or figuratively. In meditation we do not step but sit. This position is significant. We sit, as with friends or family, when we are relaxed and most ourselves. There is nothing agitated or strident or affected. We are at home. The back is held straight in an attitude of alertness, balance, and dignity. There is no need for pretence in the presence of God, but there is also no need for shame.

Robert Kiely,
Christian Meditation by those who Practice It

What I am describing here is the contemplative work of the spirit. It is this which gives God the greatest delight. For when you fix your love on him, forgetting all else, the saints and angels rejoice and hasten to assist you in every way — though the devils will rage and ceaselessly conspire to thwart you. Your fellow men are marvellously enriched by this work of yours, even if you may not fully understand how; the souls in purgatory are touched, for their suffering is eased by the effects of this work; and, of course, your own spirit is purified and strengthened by this contemplative work more than by all others put together.

Yet for all this, when God's grace arouses you to enthusiasm, it becomes the lightest sort of work there is and one most willingly done. Without his grace, however, it is very difficult and almost, I should say, quite beyond you.

Anon (fourteenth century),
The Cloud of Unknowing

The all-important aim in Christian meditation is to allow God's mysterious and silent presence within us to become more and more not only a reality, but the reality which gives meaning, shape and purpose to everything we do, to everything we are....

Sit down. Sit still and upright. Close your eyes lightly. Sit relaxed but alert. Silently, interiorly, begin to say a single word. We recommend the prayer-phrase 'Maranatha.' Recite it as four syllables of equal length. Listen to it as you say it, gently but continuously. Do not think or imagine anything — spiritual or otherwise. If thoughts and images come, these are distractions at the time of meditation, so keep returning to simply saying the word. Meditate each morning and evening for between twenty and thirty minutes.

Dom John Main (1926-82),
Word into Silence

At first this saving prayer demands hard work but if one concentrates on it with zeal it will begin to flow like a brook that murmurs in the heart. This is a mighty blessing and is well worth all the effort.

Bishop Theophane the Recluse (1815-94),
The Art of Prayer: An Orthodox Anthology

It is remarkable how the stillness and the concentration of daily meditation changes our daily lives. It is true what John Main says: 'It rearranges us in the sense that it brings all our powers and faculties into line.' It is a process of self-discovery. The mantra becomes a key that opens the door to the secret chamber of our heart. I have been very impressed by John Main's vision. In the light of Jesus' message, we are not insignificant, trivial beings. In His love and in His Spirit the call is to become the true man, the true woman.

God's call and God's hope for us is so great that we have to be most humble in order to answer. Our own realization is not to be found within our ego, but precisely by giving up the ego. Then we can share in the love and the Spirit of Christ, which actually means that we should work, eat, drink, sleep within this love and the Spirit of Christ.

It is difficult to believe that all of us are called to this fullness of life. It is difficult to realize that we all possess the liberty to accept or to refuse this fullness. It takes some time to recognize that it is precisely poverty which brings us to this fullness. In meditation, the poverty of giving up words, ideas and thoughts and the surrender to a particular word, the Mantra, makes us attentive, pure, empty and receptive to that fullness. The vision of John Main is based on the words of Jesus in the gospel, St Paul,

88

and the tradition of the early desert monks in prayer. This teaching makes us free and is addressed to everyone personally and explicitly.

Agnes D'Hooghe-Dumon,
Christian Meditation by those who Practice It

Some time ago, I was at a concert. As we waited for the concert to begin, I listened to the orchestra beginning to tune up. It was about the most discordant sound I've ever heard. Each instrument was playing its own way, in total disharmony. Then what happened was that the oboe, a quiet, little instrument, began to play and all the other instruments tuned in on its note. And gradually, all the disharmony began to calm down. Then there was silence, and the concert began. It seems to me that the mantra is very much like that little oboe. In meditation, the mantra brings all the parts of our being, one by one, bit by bit, into harmony. And when we are in harmony, we are the music of God.

Laurence Freeman,
in conversation

There are some who regard this task as so formidable and daunting that they think that it cannot be achieved without much hard and persevering preliminary work. Even then, they would say, they experience it but rarely and then only in moments of ecstasy.

I would answer such men as humbly as I can by saying that it all rests entirely on the decree and good pleasure of God, who gives every man the grace of contemplation and spiritual working according to his capacity to receive it.

There are some who will not achieve it without long and arduous spiritual labour. It will be but seldom, and then only by virtue of God's special calling, that they will experience the perfection of this work.

On the other hand there are others so attuned in grace and spirit, and so at home with God in this grace of contemplation, that they may have it when they please in the ordinary occupations of life as in sitting, walking, standing or kneeling. And, yet, during this time they have full control of their faculties and may exercise them if they wish; not, it is true, without some difficulty, but without great difficulty.

Anon (fourteenth century),
The Cloud of Unknowing

Learning to pray is learning to live as fully as possible in the present moment. In meditation we seek to enter as fully as we can into the now, and in entering into the *now* to live as fully as possible with the now-risen and the ever-loving Lord Jesus. To be thus fully committed to the present moment is to find ourselves, to enter into ourselves, to dwell within ourselves; and this we do by renouncing thought and image.

In meditation we are not thinking about the past, neither our own past nor anyone else's, nor are we thinking about the future, our own nor anyone else's. In meditation we are wholly inserted into the present, and there we live to the fullness of our capacity, our consciousness expanding as we entertain the Lord of Life. The experience of this being wholly conscious is an experience of unity and simplicity.

Dom John Main (1926-82),
The Inner Christ

We act on intuition for Otherness and the turning from egocentricity each time we enter into the practice of Christian meditation. When we are faithful to the practice of meditation, Christ's own consciousness becomes our experience. We see ourselves and our world through new eyes, the eyes of faith.

Through the use of a mantra (a repeated word), we focus our attention. Our total concentration on the mantra leads us beyond egocentricity to a place of utter stillness, a place of self-forgetfulness. The quieting of our bodies, minds, and imagination leads us to a reality beyond our own known experience.

The time spent in meditation is itself an act of faith. Nothing is supposed to happen during our prayer periods (thirty minutes each morning and evening is suggested) except that we continue to concentrate by saying our mantra. We are informed by the tradition of Christian meditation that no experience, not even what seems like religious experience, should be given our attention during this prayer time. The teachers of the practice of Christian meditation tell us to simply and gently return to repeating our mantra for the full half hour of our meditation.

Eileen O'Hea,
Woman: Her Intuition for Otherness

When we make a serious attempt to pray in spirit and in truth, we immediately become acutely conscious of our inward disintegration. In spite of all our efforts to stand before God, thoughts continue to move restlessly and aimlessly through our head, like the buzzing of flies or the capricious leaping of monkeys from branch to branch.

To contemplate means, first of all, to be present where one is — to be here and now. But usually we find ourselves unable to restrain our mind from wandering at random over time and space. We recall the past, we anticipate the future, we plan what to do next; faces and places come before us in unending succession. We lack the power to gather ourselves into the one place where we should be — here, in the presence of God; we cannot live fully in the only moment of time that truly exists — now, the immediate present. This personal disintegration is one of the most tragic consequences of the Fall.

Kallistos Ware

The mystery of the Incarnation means that the coming of Jesus has changed the basic orientation of the human condition. The human person now has the capacity to respond fully to the 'glorious might' and the 'ample power' of God through the spirit of Jesus. It is the power of response that gives each one of us the infinite capacity to be inserted into the realms of light, the capacity to be in God, to be unified, enlightened, to be utterly free within the unlimited and infinite freedom of God.

The extraordinary thing is that the way to be opened fully to this destiny is a way of utter simplicity, the way of one little word, the mantra, a way that enables us to be humble, to be poor and to be faithful.

Dom John Main (1926-82),
from a talk

The Mantra becomes one's staff of life and carries one through every ordeal.

Mahatma Gandhi (1869-1948)

Work hard then, and beat upon this high cloud of unknowing; afterwards you may rest. Anyone who takes on this work unless he be given special grace, or has been long accustomed to it, will find it hard indeed.

The demanding nature of this work is to be found in the putting down of the memory of creatures and in holding them under the cloud of forgetting. This is man's work with the help of grace. The stirring of love, that is God's work. So press on and do your part, and I promise that he will not fail in his.

Work away then. Work hard for a while and the burden will soon be lightened. For although it is hard in the beginning when you lack devotion, after a while when devotion is kindled it will become restful and light.

God will sometimes work all by himself, though not for long at a time and only when and how he wills. You will then be happily content to let him work alone.

It may be that sometimes he will send out a beam of spiritual light piercing the cloud of unknowing that is between you and him, showing you some of his secrets, of which men may not and cannot speak.

Anon (fourteenth century),
The Cloud of Unknowing

This way of simple prayer, when we are faithful to it and practice it at regular times, slowly leads us to an experience of rest and opens us to God's active presence. Moreover, we can take this prayer with us into a very busy day. When, for instance, we have spent twenty minutes in the early morning sitting in the presence of God with the words 'The Lord is my Shepherd' they may slowly build a little nest for themselves in our heart and stay there for the rest of our busy day.

Even while we are talking, studying, gardening, or building, the prayer can continue in our heart and keep us aware of God's ever-present guidance. The discipline is not directed toward coming to a deeper insight into what it means that God is called our Shepherd, but toward coming to the inner experience of God's shepherding action in whatever we think, say or do.

Henri Nouwen,
The Way of the Heart

When you have the courage to drop your defenses and sink into the inner darkness, you enter into a new experience of knowing by not knowing. After some experience of praying in silence, without words and masks, you learn to let go. You breathe more deeply, more peacefully. You can go down with ease into your inner self and joyfully stretch out your spiritual hands to grasp God who now is so close to you. It seems that you have been given new, interior eyes that lovingly gaze on him. In that silent gaze you know yourself in God's unique love for you. With new interior ears you ever so quietly listen to God as he communicates himself to you without words, images or forms.

Your prayer in such silence through the deepening of faith infused into you by the Holy Spirit brings with it a great peace because you are touching God who resides at the center of your being. Your prayer is not now something that you do, so much as an entering into a state of being. The Greek word, *enstasis*, a standing inside, best describes the prayer of the heart that unfolds in deep, interior silence. You seem to be standing inside your real self, not outside *(ecstasis),* and inside your deepest reality you are truly centered in God. You stand in his holy presence, loving him without words or images or props. The totality of your being is in a tranquil state of loving surrender.

George A. Maloney,
Alone with the Alone

Prayer is more than a matter of thinking of God; in fact, thinking of God is not even a shadow of true prayer. We do not get very far with our intellects alone. We have faculties far more suited for experiencing God in a more comprehensive way at the deeper levels of our own being. Eckhart assures us:

> This true possession of God depends on the disposition, and on an inward directing of the reason and intention toward God, not on a constant contemplation in an unchanging manner, for it would be impossible to nature to preserve such an intention, and very laborious, and not the best thing either.
>
> A man ought not to have a God who is just a product of his thought, nor should he be satisfied with that, because if the thought vanished, God too would vanish. But one ought to have a God who is present, a God who is far above the notions of men and of all created things.

At this point words are only hints or pointers to what discursive reason cannot grasp. Prayer is no longer a 'conversation with God' but becomes increasingly a simple resting in God.

Willigis Jager,
The Way to Contemplation

Unless you become as little children. What word does a child keep repeating: 'Abba, Father.' Each repetition is a new confidence established — not because the child thinks about it, but because the child experiences the relationship as real. That is what the mantra is about — no thoughts, no imagination: only presence.

Dom John Main (1926-82),
Letter, 1976

This is the formula which the mind should unceasingly cling to until, strengthened by the constant use of it and by continual meditation, it casts off and rejects the rich and full material of all manner of thoughts and restricts itself to the poverty of this one verse, and so arrives with ready ease at that beatitude of the Gospel which holds first place among the other beatitudes: for he says, 'Blessed are the poor in spirit, for theirs is the kingdom of heaven'....And so by the illumination of God himself he mounts to the manifold knowledge of him and begins henceforth to be nourished on sublimer and still more sacred mysteries.

John Cassian (AD 350-434),
The Classics of Western Spirituality

The rational mind always thinks in terms of duality; subject and object, mind and matter, body and soul, time and space. These are all categories of the rational mind.

These categories are of course valuable and necessary, for they enable us to operate within the world of time and space, the world of sense perception. We cannot discard them, but as we begin to contemplate so we go beyond these dualities. We transcend reason and logical thought, and open ourselves to the direct experience of the spirit. This is the unifying experience.

Thoughts may take us to the furthest outreach of space, but they neither find nor relate to God. God cannot be realized or known by the processes of the mind. Thought can give birth to further thoughts about God.

The hope of humanity today is to get beyond the experience of duality. A spiritual awakening in this direction is taking place all over the world. Beyond thought is where, in the words of St Paul, we find God to be 'all in all' (1 Corinthians 15:28).

Bede Griffiths (1907-93),
The Universal Christ

Today we suffer from an almost universal idolatry of giantism. It is therefore necessary to insist on the virtues of smallness. For every activity there is a certain appropriate scale, and the more active and intimate the activity, the smaller the number of people that can take part. It then becomes immediately apparent that certain things can only be taught in a very intimate circle.

E.F. Schumacher (1911-77),
Small is Beautiful

As you meditate, remember that you must have no object, no purpose, no goal, and no desire other than the experience of God-contact or God-realization. You must not have in mind any object that you wish, or any desired demonstration. You must never have in mind the healing of mind, body, lack, or fear. Never, never, must you have any goal or any object other than the attainment of God-realization and the recognition of the Presence within you.

Joel S. Goldsmith (1892-1964),
The Contemplative Life

It is helpful if you can set aside a room in your house just for meditation and nothing else, a room that will begin to have strong spiritual associations for you. Hearing that, people sometimes object, 'A separate room for meditation? I only have one room...where will I sleep? Where will I keep my clothes?' Well, if you cannot have an entire room, reserve at least one corner. But whatever you use, keep it only for meditation. Don't talk about money or possessions or frivolous things there; don't give vent to angry words. Gradually, your room or corner will become holy.

Eknath Easwaran,
Meditation

Once you begin to enter into this interior world of meditation, and to practice it as a discipline, you will realise that it is not about technique. We have become a very technique-oriented society, East and West. It is very important for us as Christians not to approach meditation as a technique, but as a discipline, as a way of learning, something to persevere in. As long as we follow it as a discipline, we will discover more and more clearly some of the things we have to give up, and some things we have to begin to do, in order to follow the path of meditation more fully, more generously and to be better disciples of the Lord.

Laurence Freeman,
from a talk

As we grow into Christian maturity we may find ourselves drawn beyond all images and concepts of God into what has been called 'the cloud of unknowing.' Here we find ourselves at the centre of a paradox, for intellectually we do not know, yet ultimately we know that which cannot be grasped by the intellect.

This has been the experience of all the mystics. Today the 'unknowing' is entered into by many who, divided by concepts, images and symbols, nevertheless are feeling a unity in God.

Bede Griffiths (1907-93),
The Universal Christ

As I understand it, all Christian prayer is a growing awareness of God in Jesus and for that growing awareness we need to come to a state of undistraction, to a state of attention and concentration — that is, to a state of awareness. And so far as I have been able to determine in the limitations of my own life, the only way that I have been able to come to that quest, to that undistractedness, to that concentration, is the way of the mantra.

Dom John Main (1926-82),
The Gethsemani Talks

Meditation has taught me how to *be*; how to *let go, let God*; how to begin by leaving self behind, with its ambitions, desires, and fears; how to walk (or stumble) in faith depending most on the power of Jesus which my touch can still draw from him. When the Angel told Joseph to fly into Egypt, he simply told him to 'Be there till I tell you.' Being where God wants us to be enables him to work powerfully through us. Is this why so much more now seems to happen, so many doors open and hands reach out, than when I was so very busy and more about my own business than my Father's?

Our daily lives are the test of the sincerity of our prayer of meditation. We cannot choose Jesus over all distractions in meditation, and then not choose him over all sin in our daily lives. In fact meditation burns out the roots of sin. The mantra which enables us to choose Jesus in meditation can also be the means whereby we choose him in all circumstances of our daily lives. So in temptation, the mantra focuses our minds on Jesus. When we are happy or grateful or want to praise God for his goodness, again the mantra comes to our aid. The mantra is our love word and so always points us to Jesus whether in praise, gratitude, or when we need help.

Monsignor Tom Fehily,
Christian Meditation by Those Who Practice It

The Abbot Pastor was consulted by one of the brothers who said, 'Many distractions come to my mind and my soul is in danger because of them.' The old man took him outside and said: 'Lift up your arms and catch the wind.' But he answered, 'I cannot.' And the old man said to him: 'If you cannot catch the wind, neither can you stop distractions from coming into your mind.'

Benedicta Ward,
Sayings of the Desert Fathers

When we meditate, we repeat the Mantra. When we start off we think that we will have this mastered in a week or two and we will be 'super' meditators. Soon, we let go of this and all expectations. We find that we can't hold the simple little Mantra. Do we get angry and give up in frustration? Or do we come to understand that prayer is a journey, a discipleship, a way?

We do not pray to be successful. We pray to be faithful. As we let go of our ambitions and desires about the Mantra, we will find that we are also letting go of many of our desires, dreams and plans for ourselves, others and God. We are getting out of the prayer 'trap' and becoming open to the God whose wisdom is beyond ours and whose love is beyond anything we could hope for or imagine.

Gerry Pierse,
A Wider Vision

I have held my soul
In peace and in silence
As a child
In its mother's arms.

This is the highest state of prayer: to be children in God's arms, silent, loving, rejoicing. And if, through this desire of ours to say something, to do something, you feel that you must open your mouth, then do this: choose one word or a little phrase which well expresses your love for him; and then go on repeating it in peace, without trying to form thoughts, motionless in love before God who is love.

And with this word or this phrase transformed into an arrow of steel, a symbol of your love, beat again and again against God's thick cloud of unknowing. Chase away even the good thoughts; they serve no purpose now.

The highest degree of contemplation one can attain in this life lies entirely in this darkness, this cloud of unknowing. With an impulse of love and a blind glance one is carried to the naked being of God himself and God alone. A blind impulse of love, fixed on God himself, which presses secretly on the cloud of unknowing is nobler and more profitable for your soul, than any other spiritual exercise.

This is my wish, a synthesis of all the gifts which the desert has made me.

Carlo Carretto (1910-89),
Letters from the Desert

Father John Main always insisted that this is a very simple, humble way. 'Quietly repeating your word,' he says, keeps the ego in its place and should lead you to the transcendent. But, unless the mantra is accompanied by faith and love, it has no real value; it would be merely a mechanism. It is a real danger merely to trust the mechanism of the mantra, but as an expression of faith and love it becomes a very powerful means to direct your faith and to open you to God.

Bede Griffiths (1907-93),
The New Creation in Christ

After you have chosen your prayer word carefully, please do not change it under any circumstances. Many people let themselves be swept away by novelty; it is part of the restlessness of our age. They will use it for six weeks and then tire of it. They change to another, and then grow weary of that one too. So they go on in this new way, new one after new, like a farmer who keeps starting a new well; they will never find water.

R.M. French (1884-1969)
The Way of a Pilgrim

It is important not to try to invent or anticipate any of the experiences. I hope that, as you come back to the discipline everyday, it will become clear that each of us is summoned to the heights of Christian prayer — each of us summoned to fullness of life. What we need however is the humility to tread the way very faithfully over a period of years so that the prayer of Christ may indeed be the grounding experience of our life.

Dom John Main (1926-82),
Moment of Christ

7
Attention and Distraction

> Block your mouth
> shut the doors of eyes and ears,
> and you will have fullness within.
> Open your mouth,
> be always busy,
> and you're beyond hope!

Lao Tzu (570-490 BC),
Tao Te Ching

Simone Weil died in 1943 at the age of thirty-three. She was serving with French Resistance forces in England at the time and trying to live on the food ration of a French workman in occupied France. Through her posthumous writings, she became a kind of apostle of the spiritual life of France during the first decade after World War II. At the heart of her insights is her definition of prayer as attention. Her French forebear, Pascal, would have approved of this for he felt that the greatest enemy, not only of prayer but also of the whole spiritual life of man, was inattention, drowsiness, complacency, what he called 'the Gethsemane sleep' referring to what the Apostles did when Jesus asked them to watch with him.

'Blessed are the drowsy ones for they shall soon drop off to sleep!' wrote Nietzsche, and his satirical warning holds for those who do not pray. For prayer is awakeness, attention, intense inward openness. In a certain way sin could be described, and described with a good deal of penetration, by noting that it is anything that destroys this attention. Pride, self-will, self-absorption, doublemindedness, dishonesty, sexual excess, overeating, overdrinking, overactivity of any sort, all destroy attention and all cut the nerve of effective prayer. Just as sleep is upset by any serious mental disturbance, so attention is dispersed when unfaced sin gets the ascendancy.

If prayer is attention, then it is naturally attention to the highest thing that I know, to my 'ultimate concern,' and this human prayer means a moving out of a life of inattention, out of the dispersion, out of 'the Gethsemane sleep' into the life of openness and attention to the highest that I know. God can only disclose the Divine whispers to those who are attending.

Douglas V. Steere,
Prayer in the Contemporary World

Wait upon God with loving and pure attentiveness, working no violence on yourself lest you disturb the soul's peace and tranquillity. God will feed your soul with heavenly food since you put no obstacle in his way.

The soul in this state must remember that if it is not conscious of making progress, it is making much more than when it was walking on foot, because God himself is bearing it in his arms. Although outwardly it is doing nothing, it is in reality doing more than if it were working since God is doing the work within it. And it is not remarkable that the soul does not see this, for our senses cannot perceive that which God works in the soul.

Let the soul then leave itself in the hands of God and have confidence in him. Let it not trust itself to the hands and works of others, for if it stays in God's care it will certainly make progress.

St John of the Cross (1542-91),
taken from *The Joy of the Saints*

One act is required — and that is all: for this one act pulls everything together and keeps everything in order....This one act is to stand with attention in your heart.

Bishop Theophane the Recluse (1815-94),
The Art of Prayer: An Orthodox Anthology

This is what you are to do: lift your heart up to the Lord, with a gentle stirring of love desiring only God and not God's gifts. Center all your attention and desire on God and let this be the sole concern of your mind and heart. Do all in your power to forget everything else, keeping your thoughts and desires free from involvement with any of God's creatures or their affairs whether in general or in particular. Perhaps this will seem like an irresponsible attitude, but I tell you, let them all be; pay no attention to them.

Anon (fourteenth century),
The Cloud of Unknowing

One disciple said: 'My master stands on one side of the river. I stand on the other holding a piece of paper. He draws a picture in the air and the picture appears on my paper. He works miracles.'

The other disciple said: 'My master works greater miracles than that,

> When he sleeps, he sleeps.
> When he eats, he eats.
> When he works, he works.
> When he meditates, he meditates.'

Zen Buddhist story

Silence is an indispensable part of the spiritual life. We need to be quiet in the presence of God. We need to sense the divine Presence not only in majestic storms, spectacular vistas of nature, powerful words, stirring music, fanfare, and applause, but also in tiny whispering sounds and in gentle, delicate stillness. The prophet Elijah stayed still long enough after the noise had subsided to recognize a quiet sign of God's presence (1 Kings 19:10-13).

Like him, we need to be silent in order to be attuned to the quiet God. We often make a lot of noise, speak a lot of words —

even to God and about God. If we would stop shouting or even talking sometime, we might hear a gentle sound of love, or simply realize that we are together with God, embraced by the divine Presence. If we are going to be aware of God, touched by God, hear God's Word, we need to be silent sometimes. We need to develop a place of solitude in our hearts.

Don Postema,
Space for God

Let the man return into his own self, and there in the centre of his soul, let him wait upon God, as one who listens to another speaking from a high tower, as though he had God in his heart, as though in the whole creation there was only God and his soul.

Peter of Alcántara (1499-1562),
Lamps of Fire

Distractions are not only inevitable, they are indispensable. And if not deliberately planned and chosen by us, they can help our prayer by leading us to realize our total dependence on God and our inability to do anything of ourselves. We must remain faithful and do what we can to stay with God even if we feel no sensible fervor.

The level-headed St Teresa of Avila wrote to a friend: 'As for the distractions you experience in reciting the Divine Office, I am subject to them as you are, and I advise you to attribute them, as I do, to weakness of the head; for Our Lord well knows that when we pray to him our intention is to pray well.'

Mary Clare Vincent
The Life of Prayer and the Way to God

The quality of attention counts for much in the quality of prayer. Warmth of heart cannot make up for it.

Simone Weil (1909-43),
Waiting for God

Don't think you can attain total awareness and whole enlightenment without proper discipline and practice. This is egomania. Appropriate rituals channel your emotions and life energy toward the light. Without the discipline to practice them, you will tumble constantly backward into the darkness.

Lao Tzu (570-490 BC),
Hua Hu Ching

It is one thing to pray with attention with the participation of the heart; it is another to descend with the mind into the temple of the heart and from there to offer mystical prayer filled with divine grace and power. The second is the result of the first. The attention of the mind during prayer draws the heart into sympathy: with the strengthening of attention, sympathy of heart and mind is turned into union of heart and mind. Finally when attention makes the prayer its own, the mind descends into the heart for the most profound and sacred service of prayer.

Jan van Ruysbroeck (1293-1381),
The Classics of Western Spirituality

Come now...
Turn aside for a while from your ordinary
employment.
Put aside your worldly cares.
Let your distractions wait.
Free yourself for a while for God
and rest in him.

Enter the inner room of your soul,
shut out everything except God
and that which can help you in seeking him.
And when you have shut the door, seek him.
Now my whole heart,
say to God
I seek your face: show me your face.

St Anselm of Canterbury (1033-1109),
Anselm of Canterbury

Truth must find an echo in the one who hears it to be recognised. Put it another way, a heart must be really listening, really wanting the truth, really wanting God.

Ruth Burrows,
Ascent to Truth

Germanus asks How is it then that, even against our will, idle thoughts steal upon us so subtly and secretly that it is fearfully hard not merely to drive them away but even to grasp and seize them? Can then a mind sometimes be found free from them and never attacked by illusions of this kind?

Moses answers It is impossible for the mind not to be approached by thoughts, but it is in the power of every earnest man either to admit them or to reject them. As then their rising up does not entirely depend on ourselves, so the rejection or admission of them lies in our power....For this purpose frequent reading and continual meditation is employed that from thence an opportunity may be provided and earnest vigils and fasts and prayers...for if these things are dropped, the mind is sure to incline in a carnal direction and fall away.

Germanus and Abba Moses (fourth century),
'A dialogue in the desert'

When you pray, you yourself must be silent. Let the prayer speak.

Tito Colliander,
The Way of the Ascetics

Silence is not merely negative — a pause between words, a temporary cessation of speech — but properly understood, it is highly positive; an attitude of attentive alertness, of vigilance, and above all of listening.

Kallistos Ware

If the heart is devoted
to the mirage of the world,

106

to the creature instead of the Creator,
the disciple is lost....

However urgently
Jesus may call us,
his call fails to find access
to our hearts.

Our hearts are closed,
for they have already been given over
to another.

Dietrich Bonhoeffer (1906-45),
'No access'

In meditation we turn within a state of silent receptivity with that open inner eye of love, that listening ear and we let our self unfold and reveal to us whatever is necessary to the *now* of our experience. We truly drink from the well of our consciousness. The water of eternal life 'gushing up' brings forth to our external world a manifestation of harmony, love, peace and health.

François C. Gerard (1924-91),
Going on a Journey

I will walk in the Presence of the Lord in the land of the living.

Psalm 116:8

And if some persons are troubled because they are no longer able thus to name God in their prayers, if they believe that God escapes them once they can no longer think of Him, should this not be attributed, rather, to their fear of escaping from themselves, as though outside this God of their conception, they might lose their identity?

The prohibition of images that God enjoined on Mount Sinai and which Deuteronomy repeats so forcibly goes well beyond images engraved on stone or wood. Let those who still doubt meditate on the Scriptures and, above all, remain in silence hearkening to the Spirit.

Henri Le Saux/Abhishiktananda (1910-73),
The Eyes of Light

Listen
The more faithfully
   you listen
   to the voice within you,
   the better
   you will hear
   what is sounding outside.

Dag Hammerskjöld (1905-61),
Markings

But how shall we find the way? What method can we devise? How can one see the inconceivable Beauty which stays within the holy sanctuary and does not come out where the profane may see It? Let him who can, follow and come within, and leave outside the sight of his eyes and not turn back to the bodily splendours which he saw before....Let all these things go, and do not look.

Plotinus (AD 204-70),
Enneads

Reminiscent of a similar question posed to Jesus, a delegation was once sent to the Buddha and asked him, 'Who are you? Are you a god?' 'I am not,' he replied. 'Well then, are you an angel?' 'I am not.' 'Are you a prophet?' they persisted. 'No,' he replied. 'Who then are you?' they asked. The Buddha replied, 'I am awake!'

Stephen J. Rossetti,
I Am Awake: Discovering Prayer

Be strong, and enter into your own body; for there your foothold is firm. Consider it well. O my heart! Go not elsewhere! Kabir says: 'Put all imaginations away, and stand fast in that which you are.'

Kabir (1440-1518),
One Hundred Poems of Kabir

Within there is a profound peace, and one experiences utter repose; and yet tatters of thought sail across the surface of consciousness like clouds across a mountaintop. In the beginning these intractable thoughts are disturbing; later on one simply lets them go their way, for they do not interfere with recollection any more than the clouds disturb the quiet of the mountain.

Willigis Jager,
The Way to Contemplation

Thoughts continue to jostle in your head like mosquitoes. To stop this jostling, you must bind the mind with one thought, or the thought of One only. An aid to this is a short prayer, which helps the mind to become simple and united....Together with the short prayer, you must keep your thought and attention turned towards God. But if you limit your prayer to words only, you are as 'sounding brass.'

Bishop Theophane the Recluse (1815-94),
The Art of Prayer: An Orthodox Anthology

8
Silence

We should endeavour to maintain
our minds in silence
remote even from such thoughts
as may seem legitimate.
Let us constantly look into the depths
of our heart saying
'Lord Jesus Christ, Son of God
Have Mercy on me.'
Recite the prayer attentively in this manner
standing, sitting or reclining
your mind into your heart
call your god with fervent desire
In patient expectation
turning away all thoughts.

Nilus Sorsky (fourteenth century)

If our life is poured out in useless words, we will never hear
anything, will never become anything; and, in the end, because
we have said everything before we had anything to say, we shall
be left speechless at the moment of our greatest decision.

But silence is ordered to that final utterance. It is not an end
in itself. Our whole life is a meditation of our last decision — the
only decision that matters. And we meditate in silence. Yet we

are bound, to some extent, to speak to others, to help them see their way to their own decision, to teach them Christ.

In teaching them Christ, our very words teach them a new silence: the silence of the Resurrection. In that silence they are formed and prepared so that they also may speak what they have heard. 'I have believed, therefore have I spoken (Ps. 115:1).

Thomas Merton (1915-68),
Thoughts in Solitude

The old man replied, 'If he is not edified by my silence, there is no hope that he will be edified by my words.'

The Sayings of the Desert Fathers

Be silent about great things
let them grow inside you
Never discuss them,
discussion is so limiting and so distracting
it makes things grow smaller
You think you swallow things
when they ought to swallow you.
Before all greatness
        be silent
        in art
        in music
        in religion
        silence.

Friedrich von Hügel (1852-1925),
The Mystical Element of Religion

People are on the lookout for ideas, and I should like to make them feel that what they need is to keep silence. The Spirit only makes himself heard by those who humbly abide in silence.

Henri Le Saux/Abhishiktananda (1910-73)

Where shall the word be found,
where will the word resound?

111

Not here, there is not enough silence
No place of grace for those who
    avoid the face
No time to rejoice for those who
walk among noise and deny the voice.

T.S. Eliot (1888-1965),
'Ash Wednesday 1930'

Every way in which the Lord helps the soul here, and all He teaches it, takes place with such quiet and so noiselessly that, seemingly to me, the work resembles the building of Solomon's temple where no sound was heard. So in this temple of God, in this His dwelling place, He alone and the soul rejoice together in the deepest silence.

St Teresa of Avila (1515-82),
The Interior Castle

Silence is more than merely the silence of noise; it is a primary reality in its own right which points to a life beyond the word and hence beyond the self.

Absence of speech does not create silence; it simply makes it more apparent. Silence is not merely the non-existence of something else, such as noise, speech, or music, as though it were only a negative condition. Silence is a formative and autonomous condition of being. Therefore it is possible to speak of silence just as it is possible to make assertions about any other positive reality.

Max Picard (1888-1965),
The World of Silence

I listen and hear the Silence
I listen and see the Silence
I listen and taste the Silence
I listen and smell the Silence
I listen and embrace the Silence

Twylah Nitsch

Of course, to begin with, silence is not silence at all; it is filled with our own perpetual inner chatter. As this gradually dies away we begin to feel we know the silence intimately, almost as a person. We may experience it as threatening, hostile, even as killing. We may experience it as boredom, tension, loneliness, insignificance, a state of being unloved, and as loss of identity.

This dark face of silence is painful to look upon, and we long to be let off the encounter. We endure the illusion of people suffering — that their suffering is different, peculiar to them, and worse than other people's. We use every trick, every device open to us to dodge the moment we dread, the moment of 'letting go,' of 'yielding, of opening ourselves to the torrents of inner pain.' Yet it is precisely this which silence must achieve.

Monica Furlong,
Contemplating Now

Be silent, everyone, in the presence of the Lord.

Zachariah 2:13

There is hardly ever a complete silence in our soul.

Frederick William Faber (1814-63),
World's Great Religious Poetry

When the mind is freed from those external reminders with which it is assaulted in every moment of its ordinary life, it gathers itself within, concentrates on the one thing necessary, and discovers in itself a clarity and transparency which otherwise is scarcely conceivable. Silence is like fasting and solitude; one has to adopt it seriously, burning one's boats, cheerfully and without looking back.

It is the same with the great inner silence — of which the former is only a sign, or at best the outer court — with the abstinence from all thoughts, the unconditional solitude of the Alone, deep within. Anyone who takes it up reluctantly, or even simply with reservations and fears, will never experience the boundless peace which it brings. Its flavour, like that of pure water or air which is so purified that it has no discernable odour, is

113

reserved for him alone who has given everything and is free from everything, in the first place from himself.

Henri Le Saux/Abhishiktananda (1910-73),
The Secret of Arunachala

Silence

I weave a silence on to my lips
I weave a silence into my mind
I weave a silence within my heart
I close my ears to distractions
I close my eyes to attractions
I close my heart to temptations.
Calm me O Lord as you stilled the storm
Still me O Lord, keep me from harm
Let all tumult within me cease
Enfold me Lord in your peace.

Celtic verses

Silence exists without speech but speech cannot exist without silence.

When the silence within the word is violated and the space between the words is obliterated, the content of the word no longer matters, for the word itself is destroyed, and the faith and hope meant to be conveyed by it are shattered. When verbal noise displaces dialogue, there is neither solitude nor community.

Unless we zealously guard the few remaining fragments of silence within our civilized life from verbal pollution and dissolution, we forfeit the redemptive intention of the word within the world.

We need to recover oases of silence within the rhyme and reason of our active life, for it is in silence that we meet God face to face.

Max Picard (1888-1965),
The World of Silence

I who live by words, am wordless when
I try my words in prayer. All language turns
To silence. Prayer will take my words and then
Reveal their emptiness. The stilled voice learns
To hold its peace, to listen with the heart
To silence that is joy, is adoration.
The self is shattered, all words torn apart
In this strange patterned time of contemplation
That, in time, breaks time, breaks words, breaks me,
And then, in silence, leaves me healed and mended.
I leave, returned to language, for I see
Through words, even when all words are ended.
     I, who live by words, am wordless when
     I turn me to the Word to pray. Amen.

Madeleine L'Engle,
The Weather of the Heart

There are times when we do not need any words or prayer, neither our own nor anyone else's and then we pray in perfect silence. This perfect silence is the ideal prayer, provided, however, that the silence is real and not daydreaming.

We have very little experience of what deep silence of body and soul means, when complete serenity fills the soul, when complete peace fills the body, when there is no turmoil or stirring of any sort and when we stand before God, completely open in an act of adoration. There may be times when we feel physically well and mentally relaxed, tired of words because we have used so many of them already; we do not want to stir and we feel happy in this fragile balance; this is on the borderline of slipping into daydreaming.

Inner silence is absence of any sort of inward stirring of thought or emotion, but it is complete alertness, openness to God. We must keep silence when we can, but never allow it to degenerate into simple contentment. To prevent this the great writers of Orthodoxy warn us never to abandon completely the normal forms of prayer, because even those who have reached this contemplative silence found it necessary, whenever they were in danger of spiritual slackness, to reintroduce words of prayer until prayer has renewed silence.

Metropolitan Anthony of Sourozh,
Creative Prayer

O Lord, my heart is not proud
nor haughty my eyes
I have not gone after things too great
nor marvels beyond me.

Truly I have set my soul
In silence and peace.
A weaned child on its mother's breast,
even so is my soul.

Psalm 131:1-2

We are what we do with silence.

Friedrich von Hügel (1852-1925),
The Mystical Element of Religion

Silence precedes speech and legitimises speech. Only a word that derives from silence has something to say. What it says is conveyed by the silence within the word.

In the beginning God spoke the first word and then gave the word to man so he could be in dialogue with his Maker about the meaning of his being. The purpose of speech is to resonate throughout creation the infinite silence behind the revealed word, thus answering that of God in everyone by naming and addressing the divine mystery which otherwise remains nameless in all its inexpressible forms as in the quiet of the dawn, the noiseless aspiration of the trees, and the silent changing of the seasons.

Max Picard (1888-1965),
The World of Silence

Silently a flower blooms,
In silence it falls away;
Yet here now, at this moment, at this place

116

the whole of the flower
the whole of the world is blooming.
This is the talk of the flower, the truth
   of the blossom;
The glory of eternal life is fully shining here.

Zenkai Shibayama,
A Flower Does Not Talk

It is in silence that God comes. When God spoke to Elias on the mountainside it was not amid the noise of the earthquake or the sound of the mighty wind or in the roar of the burning fire; it was in the calmness of the gentle breeze. And when God entered our world in human form it was 'when all things were in quiet silence.' The noises of the world must in some way be stilled if we are to hear God's voice. If we are, like Martha, 'busy about many things,' we must also learn the part that Mary played when she knelt at the feet of Christ and listened quietly to his words.

Maurice Nassan,
The Prayer of Silence

There is nothing so much like God as silence.

Meister Eckhart (1260-1327),
Sermons and Treatises

Silence is the simple stillness of the individual under the Word of God. We are silent before hearing the Word because our thoughts are already directed to the Word, as a child is quiet when he enters his father's room. We are silent after hearing the Word because the Word is still speaking and dwelling within us. We are silent at the beginning of the day because God should have the first word, and we are silent before going to sleep because the last word also belongs to God.

Silence is nothing else but waiting for God's Word and coming from God's Word with a blessing. But everybody knows that this is something that needs to be practised and learned, in these days when talkativeness prevails. Real silence, real stillness, really holding one's tongue comes only as the sober consequence of spiritual stillness.

But this stillness before the Word will exert its influence upon the whole day. If we have learned to be silent before the Word, we shall also learn to manage our silence and our speech during the day.

The silence of the Christian is listening silence, humble stillness, that may be interrupted at any time for the sake of humility.

Dietrich Bonhoeffer (1906-1945),
Modern Spirituality Series

The central silence is there
where no creature may enter, nor any idea,
and there the soul neither thinks nor acts
nor entertains any idea,
either of itself or anything else.

Meister Eckhart (1260-1327)

The father uttered one word;
that word is his Son,
and he utters him for ever in everlasting silence;
and in silence the soul has to hear it.

St John of the Cross (1542-91),
Collected Works of St John of the Cross

We cannot force grace. It is a gift. We can only wait in patience and hope, like the wise virgins. Paradoxically, it is in the waiting that God is often present. It is rare that we feel him touch our lives in the big moments. Usually, in the very depths of our being, the Spirit is working silently. Our patience and gentleness are themselves signs of this Spirit's presence.

Stephen J. Rossetti,
I Am Awake: Discovering Prayer

The world of men has forgotten the joys of silence, the peace of solitude which is necessary, to some extent, for the fullness of human living. Not all men are called to be hermits, but all men need enough silence and solitude in their lives to enable the deep inner voice of their own true self to be heard at least occasionally.

When that inner voice is not heard, when man can not attain the spiritual peace that comes from being perfectly at one with his own true self, his life is always miserable and exhausting. For he can not go on happily for long unless he is in contact with the springs of spiritual life which are hidden in the depths of his own soul.

Thomas Merton (1915-68),
The Silent Life

The
language
that God
hears best
is the
silent
language
of Love.

St John of the Cross (1542-91),
Collected Works of St John of the Cross

I can't get Galilee out of my head. To think he remained silent for thirty years. Such a silence.

Jean Sullivan (1913-1980),
Morning Light

For some people, quiet is pointless. Not talking, not hearing an undercurrent of noise (TV, conversation or radio) humming in the background, may be a vacuum into which fear, negativity or random anxiety rushes. After all, what can one 'do' without sound. A more important issue is what happens to us in silence. Silence is our perfect replica of inner poverty. Periods of silence regenerate, simplify and organize life, much as short fasts clear out and rest our digestive systems. Silence then strengthens our good will, brings peace of mind and creates for many a new life.

Marsha Sinetar,
A Way without Words

> Elected silence, sing to me
> and beat upon my whorled ear,
> pipe me to pastures still and be
> the music that I care to hear.

Gerard Manley Hopkins (1844-89),
'The habit of perfection'

St Benedict says that monks should 'diligently cultivate silence at all times.' This silence is not merely the absence of sound but is a reality in itself. How else could silence weigh heavily on a monastic environment like a blanket? If silence were nothing, there would be nothing to cultivate. To cultivate silence is to let it grow inside ourselves so that it enters every aspect of our lives.

Scripture has some impressive things to say about silence which suggest that it is important for any Christian. In Proverbs one of the basic maxims is that the wise person remains quiet while the fool talks: the wise disciple listens in order to learn the truth. St James warns us of the damage that the tongue, small as it is, can cause when it is not disciplined. More dramatically, there is the 'still small voice' which Elijah heard after the noise of the wind, earthquake, and fire. At times Jesus left the crowds and even his disciples to pray in silence. The words of Scripture, especially the Gospels, are pregnant with meaning which can penetrate to the heart only in silence. The Divine Word is utterance beyond the words of human speech. Silence is the medium through which we may perceive the depth of truth.

Brother Andrew

> Let us adore Jesus in our hearts,
> who spent thirty years out of thirty-three
> in silence;

who began his public life
by spending forty days in silence;
who often retired alone
to spend the night on a mountain in silence

Mother Teresa

Silence admits of many degrees. There can be a physical silence outside ourselves. There can be a physical silence in our various members: no speech, controlled moderaion of restless members, the hands, feet, etc. There can be various degrees of psychic silence of the emotions, the imagination, the memory, the intellect and the will. But the greatest silence is that of our spirit with God's Spirit. 'Heart speaks to heart' in silence, the language of selfsurrendering love.

This is a state of highest expanded consciousness brought about by the Holy Spirit through an increased infusion of faith, hope and love. It is the Holy Spirit alone who brings forth his gifts and fruits in your relationships with others. Your life, now rooted more deeply in the ultimate, reflects more exactly than at any earlier stage the worth of your prayer life.

Such silence in your spirit is a gift of God's spirit of love. The Holy Spirit dwelling within you teaches you how to pray deeply in your heart: 'The love of God has been poured into our hearts by the Holy Spirit who has been given us' (Rm 5:5). It is God 'who gives you his Holy Spirit' (1 Th 4:8). Our bodies through Jesus Christ have become temples of the Holy Spirit (1 Cor 6:19).

Of yourself, you are utterly incapable of praying in silence to God. Such silence is a continued process of letting go and allowing the Holy Spirit to pray within you.

George Maloney,
Alone with the Alone

He enfolds the whole universe and in silence is loving to all.

Upanishads

But if we keep silent and meek, if we listen to this silence of God, then we begin to grasp with a comprehension that exceeds our own power to evoke or even to understand why both God and the dead are so silent. Then it dawns on us that they are near us precisely in our feast of the holy souls.

God's silence is the boundless sphere where alone our love can produce its act of faith in his love. If in our earthly life his love had become so manifest to us that we would know beyond a shadow of a doubt what we really are, namely God's own beloved, then how could we prove to him the daring courage and fidelity of our love? How could such a fidelity exist at all? How could our love, in the ecstasy of faith, reach out beyond this world into his world and into his heart? He has veiled his love in the stillness of his silence so that our love might reveal itself in faith.

Karl Rahner (1904-84),
All Saints Day from the Eternal Year

I tell you that when God visits us we must be still even from prayer. When the Holy Spirit comes you must be in complete silence.

Henri Le Saux/Abhishiktananda (1910-73),
His Life Told through his Letters

> While all things were in quiet silence
> And the night was in the midst
> of its course
> Your Almighty word O Lord,
> Leapt down from your royal throne
> in Heaven.

Christmas Eve Divine Office
(Wisdom 18:14-15)

Language is so weak in explaining the fullness of the mystery. That is why the absolute silence of meditation is so supremely important. We do not try to think of God, talk to God or imagine God. We stay in that awesome silence open to the eternal silence of God. We discover in meditation, through practice and are taught daily by experience, that this is the natural ambience for all of us. We are created for this and our being flourishes and expands in that eternal silence.

Dom John Main (1926-82),
Word Made Flesh

It is in our solitude that God gives himself to us completely.

Charles de Foucauld (1858-1916),
Seeds of the Desert

The deepest level of communication is not communication, but communion. It is wordless. It is beyond words, and it is beyond speech, and it is beyond concept. Not that we discover a new unity. We discover an older unity. My dear friends, we are already one. But we imagine that we are not. What we have to recover is our original unity. What we have to be is what we are.

Thomas Merton (1915-68),
in conversation 1968

Faith has to do with what cannot be seen. But even though faith is located in the intellect, it far surpasses it; and the intellect, even when enlightened by grace, is unable to comprehend its whole mystery. At the new level to which the believer is brought by the Spirit, one can do nothing expect simply surrender to this movement which is beyond all thought and all merely intellectual realization.

It is precisely in transcending even the highest reach of the human mind, in passing beyond all symbols and expressions of itself, that faith reveals itself in its essential purity. This is the essential 'void' in which alone the human is open to and able to hear the eternal Word.

Dietrich Bonhoeffer (1906-45),
Modern Spirituality Series

Contemplative reading of the holy scriptures and silent time in the presence of God belong closely together. The word of God draws us into silence; silence makes us attentive to God's word. The word of God penetrates through the thick of human verbosity to the silent centre of our heart: silence opens in us the space where the word can be heard. Without reading the word silence becomes stale, and without silence, the word loses its recreative power.

The word leads to silence and silence to the word. The word is born in silence and silence is the deepest response to the word.

Henri Nouwen,
Reaching Out

Our dead imitate this silence. Thus, through silence, they speak to us clearly. They are nearer to us than through all the audible words of love and closeness. Because they have entered into God's life, they remain hidden from us....They live in his life. They speak the word of God of the true life, the word that is far removed from our dying. The dead are silent because they live.

Karl Rahner (1904-84),
All Saints Day from the Eternal Year

Sing, rejoice, daughter of Zion; for I am coming to dwell in the middle of you — it is the Lord who speaks. Many nations will join the Lord on that day; they will become his people...

Let all mankind be silent before the Lord, he is awakening and is coming from his holy dwelling.

Zachariah 2:14-15, 17

Most important, silence leads us into the reality of God. The noise around and within us tightens us, makes us smaller. (Our muscles contract when they are tense.) Silence opens us up. It creates the space in our minds and hearts to receive the Word of God. We discover how we tend to distort everything around us, that we even use our ideas about God to fit our own fantasies. But when we give ourselves to silence, we find that God begins to reach us in a new way. God is not someone who stands aside and simply imposes commands on us. No. God enters into the depths of our being where his own image is to be found. We can experience God's love in us so deeply that our way of living is transformed.

The more silence has a home in us, the more freedom we have from whatever noise our environment brings us. Silence does not even need to wait for the noise to stop. Silence enters the noise and waits with infinite patience. Silence teaches us the patience which frees us from the hold noise has over us. Silence invites us to share in that freedom which is the freedom of God.

Brother Andrew

In silence man can most readily preserve his integrity.

Meister Eckhart (1260-1327),
Sermons and Treatises

Persons of deep prayer learn to live in this silent recollection, focused upon God as the center of their being. You too can learn to descend to the innermost ground of your being by letting go, by conquering the noise of your own state of limited consciousness whereby you control your life, and letting God become the guide of your life. Through levels of consciousness you sink into the 'cloud of unknowing,' that state of surrender to God within which the untapped regions beneath the habitual surface of your existence are turned over to God's healing love and control.

George A. Maloney,
Alone with the Alone

If we hope to move beyond the superficialities of our culture — including our religious culture — we must be willing to go down into the recreating silence, into the inner world of contemplation.

Richard Foster,
Celebration of Discipline

We need to find God, and he cannot be found in noise and restlessness. God is the friend of silence. See how nature — trees, flowers, grass — grow in silence; see the stars, the moon and sun, how they move in silence. Is not our mission to give God to the poor in the slums? Not a dead God, but a living, loving God. The more we receive in silent prayer, the more we can give in our active life. We need silence to be able to touch souls. The essential thing is not what we say, but what God says to us and through us. All our words will be useless unless they come from within — words which do not give the light of Christ increase the darkness.

Mother Teresa,
Something Beautiful for God

Silence is the essential human response to the mystery of God, to the infinity of God.

Dom John Main (1926-82),
Moment of Christ

And it is for this very reason that there must always be in the Church ministers divested of all human means — of culture, of wealth, of prestige, rich only in their indigence — the saintly parish priest of Ars can serve as model and patron — and also ministers whose diaconia is to observe silence and to transmit the experience through the ministry of silence. They are supreme witnesses of the Spirit and also serve as a reminder to the world and to Christians that in the domain of things of God, only the Spirit is efficacious.

Henri Le Saux/Abhishiktananda (1910-73),
The Eyes of Light

St John of the Ladder advises: 'Let the memory of Jesus combine with your breath — then will you know the profit of silence.' Another teaches: 'A monk should have memory of God in place of breath' or, as another says: 'One's love of God should run before breathing.'

Gregory of Sinai (fourteenth century),
taken from *The Art of Prayer: An Orthodox Anthology*

A distinguished archaeologist spent a few years amongst the natives of the Upper Amazon. He once attempted a forced march through the jungle. The party made very good progress for the first few days, but on the third morning, when it was time to start, the natives just sat without moving, looking very solemn and made no preparation to leave.

The Chief explained to the archaeologist the problem, 'They can't move any further until their souls have caught up to their bodies.' Those natives were intelligent. They had discovered something we often forget — the need to rest in silence from time to time and indeed let our souls catch up to our bodies.

Anon (Readers Digest)

God cannot be thought, cannot be expressed. God is. The possession of God is the silence of the heart. The thought of God is the silence of the mind.

Mother Mary of St Austin

Anyone who thinks that his time is too valuable to spend keeping quiet will eventually have no time for God and his brother, but only for himself and for his own follies.

Dietrich Bonhoeffer (1906-45),
The Cost of Discipleship

Silence is the language of deeper, infused prayer that the Holy Spirit gives to God's poor children who hunger and thirst for his word. Ultimately it is the ability to live in mystery. For those who enter into this mystery, there is real communication, deep love, full healing and maturity.

But how few are ready to pay the price to enter deeply into mystery and stay there! Prayer is a mystery; silence is its language. To enter into a successful retreat in order to surrender each moment to God's holy will, you need at each moment to want to live in the atmosphere of inner silence which is the same as poverty of spirit or true humility.

George Maloney,
Alone with the Alone

Now concentration is only possible in a condition of calm and silence, at the expense of the automatism of thought and imagination.

The 'to be silent' therefore precedes the 'to know,' the 'to will' and the 'to dare.' This is why the Pythagorean school prescribed five years silence to beginners or 'hearers.' One dared to speak there only when one 'knew' and 'was able to,' after having mastered the art of being silent — that is to say, the art of concentration.

The prerogative 'to speak' belonged to those who no longer spoke automatically, driven by the game of the intellect and imagination, but who were able to suppress it owing to the practice of interior and exterior silence, and who knew what they were saying — again thanks to the same practice. The silentium practised by Trappist monks and prescribed for the time of 'retreat,' generally to all those there who are taking part, is only the application of the same true law.

Anonymous spiritual writer,
Meditations on the Tarot

Through God's one Word, St John writes in his prologue, all of creation is brought into existence. Mountains and oceans, birds and beasts, flowers and grains tumble forth in profuse richness from the finger tips of the creating God — and all is done in silence!

When we can withdraw from our busy, fragmented worlds that pull us into so many directions, filling us with frustrations and anxieties, and enter into God's silence found in all of primeval nature, then we are opening ourselves up to deep healing. When we enter into the primeval, endless now of God's quiet, we enter into a state of being. It is hardly a state of passivity or idleness. It is beyond pragmatic descriptions. It is where life and love merge into the same experience.

George A. Maloney,
Alone with the Alone

I look at him, he looks at me, and we are happy.

An old peasant talking about prayer
to the Curé of Ars (1788-1859)

Christ's existence was ruled by a great silence. His soul was listening. It was given over to the needs of others. In his innermost being he was silent, not asserting himself, detached. He did not grasp at anything in the world. Thus he overcame in His life the power of habit and routine, of dullness and fatigue, and created within Himself a carefree tranquillity, a place for every encounter. He was unreservedly receptive.

Ladislaus Boros (1927-1981),
Being a Christian Today

I learn hereby of a work that is invisible and seems like rest. How few know of a teaching that is silence; of a work that is not work, and is peace.

Lao Tzu (570-490 BC)
Tao Te Ching

How can you expect God to speak in that gentle and inward voice which melts in the soul, when you are making so much noise with your rapid reflections? Be silent, and God will speak again.

François Fénelon (1651-1718),
Christian Perfection

I am the Way, and the Master who watches in silence; thy friend and thy shelter and thy abode of peace. I am the beginning and the middle and the end of all things; their seed of Eternity, their Treasure supreme.

Bhagavad Gita

The last words of St. Thomas: 'All that I have written seems to me nothing but straw...compared to what I have seen and what has been revealed to me' — emphasized the centrality of silence and of the unknowable.

The last word of St Thomas is not communication but silence. And it is not death which takes the pen out of his hand. His tongue is stilled by the superabundance of life in the mystery of God. He is silent, not because he has nothing further to say; he is silent because he has been allowed a glimpse into the inexpressible depths of that mystery which is not reached by any human thought or speech.

Joseph Pieper,
The Silence of St Thomas

The first time Rabbi Mendel, the son of the zaddik of Vorki, met Rabbi Eleazar, the grandson of the maggid of Koznitz, the two retired to a room. They seated themselves opposite each other and sat in silence for a whole hour. Then they admitted the others. 'Now we are ready,' said Rabbi Mendel.

Martin Buber (1878-1965),
Tales of the Hasidim

If even you hear the sound of wind through the reeds, you are not yet in silence.

Arsenius Autorianus (thirteenth century)

The Lord is in his holy temple;
let all the earth keep silence before him.

Habakkuk 2:20

Out of the silence a secret word was spoken to me. Ah sir: what is this silence and where is that word spoken? We shall say, as I have heretofore, (it is spoken) in the purest element of the soul, in the soul's most exalted place, in the core, yes, in the essence of the soul. The central silence is there, where no creature may enter, nor any idea, and there the soul neither thinks nor acts nor entertains any idea, either of itself or of anything else.

In Being...there is no action and, therefore, there is none in the soul's essence. The soul's agents, by which it acts, are derived from the core of the soul. In that core is the central silence, the pure peace, and abode of the heavenly birth, the place for this event: this utterance of God's word. By nature the core of the soul is sensitive to nothing but the divine Being, unmediated. Here God enters the soul with all he has and not in part. He enters the soul through its core and nothing may touch that core except God himself.

Meister Eckhart (1260-1327),
Sermons and Treatises

The Word proceeds from Silence as Ignatius, the great bishop of Antioch, taught. And it is only in the silence of the Spirit that the Voice can be heard. Only the Spirit can make the Word be understood, as Jesus affirmed. When the Voice became silent on the earth, the Spirit appeared in tongues of fire on the heads and in the hearts of the disciples. The knowledge and the mystery of God is transmitted only by means beyond words.

Henri Le Saux/Abhishiktananda (1910-73),
The Eyes of Light

Silence is especially important if I want to learn to pray. For prayer at least at its deepest level is not so much conversation with God, but my silence communing with the silence of God. In this silent encounter I experience that God is ALL and that apart from God I am nothing.

William Shannon,
Seeking the Face of God

Love silence above everything else, for it brings you near to fruit which the tongue is too feeble to expound. First of all we force ourselves to be silent, but then from out of our silence something else is born that draws us into silence itself. May God grant you to perceive that which is born of silence! If you begin in this discipline I do not doubt how much light will dawn in you from it.

After a time a certain delight is born in the heart as a result of the practice of this labour, and it forcibly draws the body on to persevere in stillness. A multitude of tears is born in us by this discipline, at the wondrous vision of certain things which the heart

131

perceives distinctly, sometimes with pain, and sometimes with wonder. For the heart becomes small and becomes like a tiny babe: as soon as it clings to prayer, tears burst forth.

> St Isaac of Syria (sixth century),
> taken from *The Joy of the Saints*

Solitude is not found so much by looking outside the boundaries of your dwelling as by staying within them. Solitude is not something you must hope for in the future. Rather, it is a deepening of the present; and unless you look for it in the present, you will never find it.

> Thomas Merton (1915-68),
> *The Sign of Jonas*

With silence one irritates the Devil.

> Bulgarian proverb

You discover in the silence that you are loved, that you are lovable. It is the discovery that everyone must make in their lives if they are going to become fully themselves, fully human.

> Dom John Main (1926-82),
> *Moment of Christ*

Anyone who is really possessed of the word of Jesus can listen to his silence and so be perfect; so that he may act through his words and be known by his silence.

> St Ignatius of Antioch (first century AD),
> *The Apostolic Fathers*

Abbot Pastor said: Any trial whatever that comes to you can be conquered by silence.

> Thomas Merton (1915-68),
> *Wisdom of the Desert*

Silence is as dangerous as speech, if you are attached to it, for silence is likewise only a sign, and the 'one thing' (needful) is beyond silence.

> Henri Le Saux/Abhishiktananda (1910-73),
> *His Life Told through his Letters*

Speech is the organ of the present world. Silence is the mystery of the world to come.

> St Isaac of Syria (sixth century),
> taken from *The Joy of the Saints*

True silence is the search of man for God. True silence is a suspension bridge that a soul in love with God builds to cross the dark, frightening gullies of its own mind, the strange chasms of temptation, the depthless precipices of its own fears that impede its way to God.

True silence is a key to the immense and flaming heart of God. It is the beginning of a divine courtship that will end only in the immense, creative, fruitful, loving silence of final union with the Beloved.

Such silence is holy, a prayer beyond all prayers, leading to the final prayer of constant presence of God, to the heights of contemplation, when the soul, finally at peace, lives by the will of him whom she loves totally, utterly, and completely.

> Catherine de Hueck Doherty (1896-1985),
> *Poustinia*

Silence can be terribly threatening to people in the transistorized culture that we live in.

> Dom John Main (1926-82),
> *Moment of Christ*

Being quiet in the presence of God is difficult. Silence and solitude ask for much discipline and risk taking because we always seem to have something more urgent to do and just sitting there and doing nothing often disturbs us more than it helps. But there is no way around this. Being useless and silent in the presence of our God belongs to the core of all prayer. In the beginning we often hear our own unruly inner noises more loudly than God's voice. This is at times very hard to tolerate.

But slowly, very slowly, we discover that the silent time makes us quiet and deepens our awareness of ourselves and God. Then, very soon, we start missing these moments when we are deprived of them, and before we are fully aware of it an inner momentum has developed that draws us more and more into silence and closer to that still point where God speaks to us.

Henri Nouwen,
Reaching Out

Silence is the folding of the wings of the intellect to open the door of the heart.

Catherine de Hueck Doherty (1896-1985)
Poustinia

Inner silence is not a forced attitude to create a kind of emptiness within. It consists of abandoning ourselves to Christ.

Brother Roger of Taize
Easter Letter 1994

Interior silence — the inner stillness to which meditation leads — is where the Spirit secretly anoints the soul and heals our deepest wounds.

St. John of the Cross (1541-1591)
Collected Works of St. John of the Cross

9
The Spiritual Journey

Look at the empty, wealthy night
The pilgrim moon!
I am the appointed hour,
The 'now' that cuts
Time like a blade.
I am the unexpected flash,
Beyond 'yes' and 'no,'
The forerunner of the Word of God.

Follow my ways and I will lead you,
To golden-haired suns,
Logos and Music, blameless joys,
Innocent of Questions
And beyond answers.

For I, Solitude, am thine own self:
I, Nothingness, am thy All.
I, Silence, am thy Amen!

Thomas Merton (1915-68),
'Zen and the birds of appetite'

My little way is the way of spiritual childhood, the way of trust
and absolute self-surrender. In my little way everything is most

135

ordinary, for all I do must likewise be within everyone's reach.

Do not think that I am overwhelmed with consolations. Far from it! My joy consists in being deprived of all joy here on earth. Jesus does not guide me openly; I neither see nor hear him. Nor is it through books that I learn, for I do not understand what I read. Yet at times I am consoled by some chance words, such as the following which I read after a meditation passed in utter dryness: the Lord said to St Margaret Mary: 'Here is the master I give you. He will teach you all that you should do. I wish to make you read in the Book of Life in which is contained the science of love.'

St Thérèse of Lisieux (1873-1897),
Daily Readings with St. Thérèse

That devotee who looks upon friend and foe with equal regard, who is not buoyed up by praise nor cast down by blame, alike in heat and cold, pleasure and pain, free from selfish attachments, the same in honor and dishonor, quiet, ever full, in harmony everywhere, firm in faith — such a one is dear to me.

Bhagavad Gita

Is Eckhart, the recollected, the withdrawn, suggesting that silent, solitary meditation is a waste of time? The answer to this question, as always with a paradoxical thinker like Eckhart, is yes and no. Insofar as meditation can help us to acquire an inner state of concentration and awareness of God in the core of the Self, it is very far from being a waste of time. But if, having acquired that state, we want to remain forever enjoying it in silence and solitude, ignoring our worldly affairs and responsibilities, we are wasting our time, and deluding ourselves very seriously. We have failed to grasp what union with God, knowledge of God, really is....

The spiritual life...is rather a matter of self-abandonment, of freedom and openness, of not clinging to anything, of not refusing anything. This freedom is what we should aim at perpetually. Fixated on the outer world, we retreat into the inner; fixated on the inner, we turn again to the outer. By breaking down the barriers of clinging, we break down the barriers of self-will, and these, once down, allow the awareness of God to stream into our minds without hindrance. God is then present to us everywhere, both in and out of meditation.

Cyprian Smith,
The Way of Paradox

For this commandment which I command thee this day, it is not hidden from thee, neither is it far off.

It is not in heaven, that thou shouldest say, Who shall go up for us to heaven and bring it unto us, that we may hear it, and do it?

Neither is it beyond the sea, that thou shouldest say, Who shall go over the sea for us, and bring it unto us, that we may hear it, and do it?

But the word is very nigh unto thee, in thy mouth, and in thy heart, that thou mayest do it.

Deuteronomy 30:11-14

In one sense we are always travelling, and travelling as if we did not know where we were going. In another sense we have already arrived.

Thomas Merton (1915-68),
The Seven-Storey Mountain

Falsehood turns from the way; truth goes all the way; the end of the way is truth; the way is paved with truth. The sage travels there without desire.

Truth lies beyond imagination, beyond paradise; great, smaller than the smallest; near, further than the furthest; hiding from the traveller in the cavern.

Nor can penance discover Him, nor ritual reveal, nor eye see, nor tongue speak; only in meditation can mind, grown pure and still, discover formless truth.

Mundaka Upanishad

To discover God
is not to discover an idea

but to discover oneself.
It is to awaken
to that part of one's existence
which has been hidden from sight
and which one has refused to recognize.

The discovery may be very painful;
it is like going through
a kind of death.

But it is the one thing
which makes life
worth living.

Bede Griffiths (1907-93),
'Awakening'

Faith is the experience of divine breath; hope is the experience of divine light; and love is the experience of divine fire. There is no authentic and sincere religious life without faith, hope and love; but there is no faith, hope and love without mystical experience or, what is the same thing, without grace. No intellectual argument can awaken faith; what it can do, at best, is to eliminate obstacles, misunderstandings and prejudices, and thus help to establish the state of interior silence necessary for the experience of the divine breath. But faith itself is the divine breath whose origin is found neither in logical reasoning, nor in aesthetic impression, nor in human moral action.

The divine and flaming Word shines in the world of the silence of the soul and 'moves' it. This movement is living faith — therefore real and authentic — and its light is hope or illumination.

Anonymous spiritual writer,
Meditations on the Tarot

People of Athens...
as I walked through your city
and looked at the places
where you worship,
I found...

an altar on which is written,

To an Unknown God.

That which you worship...
even though you do not know it,
is what I now proclaim to you.

God who made the world
and everything in it,
is Lord of heaven and earth,
and does not live in temples
made by men...

It is he himself
who gives life and breath and
everything else to men...
In him we live and move and are.

Acts of the Apostles 17:22-5, 28)

A very hard day. But I keep finding myself in prayer. And that is something I shall always be able to do, even in the smallest space: pray. And I know for certain that there will be a continuity between the life I have led and the life about to begin. Because my life is increasingly an inner one and the outer setting matters less and less.

Truly my life is one long hearkening unto my self and unto others, unto God. And if I say that I hearken, it is really God who hearkens inside me. The most essential and the deepest in me hearkening unto the most essential and deepest in the other. God to God.

But I refresh myself from day to day at the original source, life itself, and I rest from time to time in prayer. And what those who say, 'You live too intensely,' do not know is that one can withdraw into a prayer as into a convent cell and leave again with renewed strength and with peace regained.

I often walk with a spring in my step along the barbed wire and then time and again it soars straight from my heart — I can't help it, that's just the way it is, like some elementary force — the feeling that life is glorious and magnificent, and that one day we shall be building a whole new world. Against every new outrage and every fresh horror we shall put up one more piece of love and goodness, drawing strength from within ourselves. We may suffer, but we must not succumb.

In the past I, too, used to be one of those who occasionally exclaimed, 'I really am religious, you know.' Or something like that. But now I sometimes actually drop to my knees beside my bed, even on a cold winter night. And I listen in to myself, allow myself to be led, not by anything on the outside, but by what wells up from deep within. It's still no more than a beginning. I know. But it is no longer a shaky beginning, it has already taken root.

For once you have begun to walk with God, you need only keep on walking with Him and all of life becomes one long stroll.

Etty Hillesum (1914-43),
An Interrupted Life

No need to recall the past, no need to think about what was done before. See, I am doing a new deed, even now it comes to light; can you not see it? Yes, I am making a road in the wilderness, paths in the wilds.

Isaiah 43:18-19

The highest good is like water.
Water gives life to the ten thousand things
    and does not strive.
It flows in places men reject and so is like
    the Tao.
In dwelling, be close to the land.
In meditation, go deep in the heart.
In dealing with others, be gentle and kind.
In speech, be true.
In ruling, be just.
In business, be competent.
In action, watch the timing.
No fight; no blame.

Lao Tzu (570-490 BC),
Tao Te Ching

Brothers, have no fear of men's sin. Love a man even in his sin, for that is the semblance of divine love, and is the highest love on earth. Love all god's creation, the whole and every grain of sand in it. Love every leaf and every ray of God's light. Love the animals, love the plants, love everything. If you love everything you will perceive the divine mystery in things. Once you perceive it, you will begin to comprehend it better every day. And you will come at last to love the whole world with an all embracing love.

Fyodor Dostoevsky (1821-81),
The Brothers Karamazov

How well I know that flowing spring
   in black of night.
The eternal fountain is unseen
How well I know where she has been
   in black of night.

St John of the Cross (1541-91),
'The fountain'

I pray that the God of our Lord Jesus Christ, the all glorious Father, may give you the spiritual powers of wisdom and vision, by which there comes the knowledge of Him. And I pray that your inward eyes may be illumined, so that you may know what is the hope to which He calls you.

Ephesians 1:16-18

The purpose of a fish trap is to catch fish, and
   when the fish are caught, the trap is forgotten.
The purpose of a rabbit snare is to catch rabbits.
When the rabbits are caught, the snare is forgotten.
The purpose of words is to convey ideas. When the
   ideas are grasped, the words are forgotten.
Where can I find a man who has forgotten words?
He is the one I would like to talk to.

Chuang Tzu (369-286 BC),
The Way of Chuang Tzu

With all this in mind then, I kneel in prayer to the Father, from whom every family, in heaven and on earth takes its name. That out of the treasures of His glory He may grant you strength and power throughout His Spirit in your inner being; that through faith, Christ may dwell in your hearts in love, with deep roots and firm foundations. May you be strong to grasp with all God's people, what is the breadth and length and height and depth of the love of Christ and to know it, though it is beyond knowledge. So may you attain to fullness of being, the fullness of God Himself.

Ephesians 3:14-19

You must go by a way wherein is no ecstasy.
In order to arrive at what you do not know.
You must go by a way which is the way of ignorance.
In order to possess what you do not possess
You must go by the way of dispossession.
In order to arrive at what you are not
You must go through the way in which you are not.
And what you do not know is the only thing you know
and what you own is what you do not own
And where you are is where you are not.

T.S. Eliot (1888-1965),
Four Quartets

All the way to Heaven is Heaven. (Because Jesus is the way.)

St Catherine of Siena (1347-80),
The Classics of Western Spirituality

Ah! do let us stay very far from all that is brilliant. Let us love our littleness, love to feel nothing; then we shall be poor in spirit — and Jesus will come for us far off as we are. He will transform us...

St Thérèse of Lisieux (1873-97),
The Autobiography of St Thérèse of Lisieux

Truth has to appear only once, in one single mind, for it to be impossible for anything ever to prevent it from spreading universally and setting everything ablaze.

Pierre Teilhard de Chardin (1881-1955),
The Heart of Matter

We can easily forgive a child who is afraid of the dark;
the real tragedy is when men are afraid of the light.

Plato (428-345 BC),
Plato: Works

As he was dying, Abba Benjamin taught his sons this: Do this, and you'll be saved: Rejoice always, pray constantly, and in all circumstances give thanks.

Yushi Nomura,
Sayings from the Desert Fathers

Thus, throughout the centuries, O great Lover,
   you have drawn so many
   to your Temple, to your caves,
   to your rocky peak, crowned with Flame,
   to your springs of living water;
thus you draw to yourself so many, panting,
   falling prostrate at your feet,
   lost in the cave of your heart,
and there you keep them, sighing, groaning,
   shuddering as they cry out for your Grace!

Upanishads

I urge you, then, pursue your course relentlessly. Attend to tomorrow and let yesterday be. Never mind what you have gained so far. Instead reach out to what lies ahead. If you do this you will remain in the truth. For now, if you wish to keep growing you

143

must nourish in your heart the lively longing for God. Though this loving desire is certainly God's gift, it is up to you to nurture it....Press on then. I want to see how you fare. Our Lord is always ready. He awaits only your cooperation.

Anon (fourteenth century),
The Cloud of Unknowing

We shall not cease from exploration
And the end of all our exploring
Will be to arrive where we started
And know the place for the first time.
Through the unknown, remembered gate
When the last of earth left to discover
Is that which was the beginning,
At the source of the longest river
The voice of the hidden waterfall
And the children in the apple tree
Not known, because not looked for
But heard, half-heard, in the stillness
Between two waves of the sea.

Quick now, here, now, always —
A condition of complete simplicity
(Costing not less than everything)
And all shall be well and
All manner of things shall be well
When the tongues of flame are infolded
Into the crowned knot of fire
And the fire and the rose are one.

T.S. Eliot (1888-1965),
Four Quartets

Every man has two journeys to make through life. There is the outer journey, with its various incidents and the milestones....There is also an inner journey, a spiritual Odyssey, with a secret history of its own.

William R. Inge (1860-1954),
Christian Mysticism

For me to be a saint means to be myself. Therefore the problem of sanctity and salvation is in fact the problem of finding out who I am and of discovering my true self.

Trees and animals have no problem. God makes them what they are without consulting them, and they are perfectly satisfied.

With us it is different. God leaves us free to be whatever we like. We can be ourselves or not, as we please. We are at liberty to be real, or to be unreal. We may wear now one mask and now another, and never, if we so desire, appear with our own true face.

We are free beings and sons of God. We are called to share with God the work of creating the truth of our identity. We can evade this responsibility by playing with masks, and this pleases us because it can appear at times to be a free and creative way of living.

It is quite easy, it seems to please everyone. But in the long run the cost and the sorrow come very high.

To work out our own identity in God...demands close attention to reality at every moment. Unless I desire this identity and work to find it with Him and in Him, the work will never be done.

Thomas Merton (1915-68),
The Shining Wilderness

Speaking to
the Little Prince
about love and life,
the Fox says:
And now here
is my secret,
a very simple secret.
It is only
with the heart
that one can see rightly;
What is essential
is invisible
to the eye.

Antoine de Saint-Exupéry (1900-44),
The Little Prince

I stepped down into the most hidden depth of my being, lamp in hand and ears alert, to discover whether in the deepest recesses of the blackness within me I might not see the glint of the waters of the current that flows on, whether I might not hear the murmur of the mysterious waters that rise from the uttermost depths, and will burst forth no man knows where. With terror and intoxicating emotion, I realised that my poor trifling existence was one with the immensity of all that is and all that is in the process of becoming.

Pierre Teilhard de Chardin (1881-1955),
The Hymn of the Universe

I fled Him, down the nights and down the days;
   I fled Him, down the arches of the years;
I fled Him, down the labyrinthine ways
   Of my own mind; and in the midst of tears
I hid from Him, and under running laughter.

   Up vistaed hopes I sped;
   And shot, precipitated.
Adown Titanic glooms of chasmed fears,
   From those strong Feet that followed, followed after.

   But with unhurrying chase,
   And unperturbed pace,
Deliberate speed, majestic instancy,
   They beat — and a Voice beat
   More instant that the Feet —
'All things betray thee, who betrayest Me.'

Francis Thompson (1859-1907),
'The Hound of Heaven'

Two men went up to the Temple to pray, one a Pharisee, the other a tax-collector. The Pharisee stood there and said this prayer to himself, 'I thank you, God, that I am not grasping, unjust, adulterous like the rest of mankind, and particularly that I am not like this tax-collector here. I fast twice a week; I pay tithes on all I get.' The tax-collector stood some distance away, not daring even to raise his eyes to heaven; but he beat his breast and said, 'God, be merciful to me, a sinner.' This man, I tell you, went home again at rights with God; the other did not. For everyone who exalts himself will be humbled, but the man who humbles himself will be exalted.

Luke 18:10-14

If you attempt to gaze on it directly, you are blinded and enter into a darkness that is your own, not God's. God knows this, and devised for our sake certain precautionary measures. Christ knew it, and issued his tense warning. 'Unless you change and become like little children you will never enter the kingdom of heaven' (Mt 18:3)....

There is one way, and one only, of coming through the experience: the way of childhood, littleness, humility, persevering prayer, tears. It is not easy, I admit, because before resolving to become little we are only too inclined to try every other way imaginable. In nearly every case the way of humility and tears is chosen only when one feels defeated and at a loss where to turn.

The parable of the wedding feast described by Luke tells how, in order to have his table full, the king finally commands his servants, 'Go to the open roads and the hedgerows and force people to come in...' (Lk 14:23). And it is sad to think that we possibly begin to search for God only because we no longer know where else to go, and only when, let down by beauty, by health and by our dreams, we are prepared to open ourselves to the One who still loves us, and makes use of our misfortunes to compel us to enter at last into the kingdom of his love.

Carlo Carretto (1910-89),
In Search of the Beyond

Possessing all because possessing nothing,
knowing all because knowing nothing,
enjoying all because enjoying nothing,
being all because being nothing.

St John of the Cross (1542-91),
Collected Works of St John of the Cross

The world's spiritual geniuses seem to discover that the mind's muddy river, this ceaseless flow of trivia and trash, cannot be dammed, and that trying to dam it is a waste of effort that might lead to madness. Instead you must allow the muddy river to flow unheeded in the dim channels of consciousness; you raise your sights: you look along it, mildly, acknowledging its presence without interest and gazing beyond it into the realm of the real where subjects and objects act and rest purely without utterance.

Annie Dillard,
Pilgrim at Tinker Creek

He 'prays without ceasing.' It is given him 'always to pray, and not to faint.' Not that he is always in the house of prayer, though he neglects no opportunity of being there. Neither is he always on his knees, although he often is, or on his face, before the Lord his God. Nor yet is he always crying aloud to God, or calling upon him in words. For many times 'the Spirit maketh intercession for him with groans that cannot be uttered.'

But at all times the language of his heart is this: 'Thou brightness of the eternal glory, unto thee is my heart, though without a voice, and my silence speaketh unto thee.' And this is true prayer, and this alone. But his heart is ever lifted up to God, at all times and in all places.

In this he is never hindered, much less interrupted, by any person or thing. In retirement or company, in leisure, business, or conversation, his heart is ever with the Lord. Whether he lie down or rise up, God is in all his thoughts. He walks with God continually, having the loving eye of his mind still fixed upon him, and everywhere 'seeing him that is invisible.'

John Wesley (1703-91),
taken from *The Joy of the Saints*

If when we plunge our hand
    into a bowl of water,
Or stir up the fire with the bellows
Or tabulate interminable columns of figures
    on our book-keeping table,
Or, burnt by the sun, we are plunged in

148

the mud of the rice-field,
Or standing by the smelter's furnace
We do not fulfill the same religious life
    as if in prayer in a monastery,
    the world will never be saved.

Mahatma Gandhi (1869-1948)

In the waste lands he adopts him, in the howling desert of the wilderness. He protects him, rears him, guards him as the pupil of his eye. Like an eagle watching its nest, hovering over its young, he spreads out his wings to hold him, he supports him on his pinions.

Deuteronomy 32:10-11

Upon a gloomy night,
With all my cares to loving ardours flushed,
(O venture of delight!)
With nobody in sight
I went abroad when all my house was hushed.

In safety, in disguise,
In darkness up the secret stair I crept,
(O happy enterprise!)
Concealed from other eyes
When all my house at length in silence slept.

Upon the lucky night
In secrecy, inscrutable to sight,
I went without discerning
And with no other light
Except for that which in my heart was burning....

Lost to myself I stayed
My face upon my lover having laid
From all endeavour ceasing:
And all my cares releasing

Threw them amongst the lilies there to fade.

St John of the Cross (1542-91),
Poems of St John of the Cross (Abridged)

The truest solitude is not something outside you, not an absence of men or of sound around you; it is an abyss opening up in the center of your own soul. And this abyss of interior solitude is created by a hunger that will never be sampled with any created things.

Thomas Merton (1915-68),
Seeds of Contemplation

Sarapion the Sindonite travelled once on a pilgrimage to Rome. Here he was told of a celebrated recluse, a woman who lived always in one small room, never going out. Skeptical about her way of life — for he was himself a great wanderer — Sarapion called on her and asked, 'Why are you sitting here?' To which she replied, 'I am not sitting; I am on a journey.'

The Desert Fathers,
taken from *The Joy of the Saints*

From the infinity of space and time the infinitely more finite love of God comes to court us. He comes at his own time. We can only choose to accept and welcome him or to reject him....If we are willing, God plants a little seed in us and goes away. From that moment God has nothing more to do, nor we either, except to wait. We must only never regret saying yes to him, our nuptial yes. This is not as simple as it sounds, because the growth of the seed within us is painful.

Indeed in order to allow it to grow, we cannot but destroy whatever puts obstacles in its way; that is, pluck up the under-growth and the weeds...the gardening to be done has to be violent. Still the seed, independent of the gardening, does grow by itself. One day the time will come when the soul belongs to God; that day the soul will not only agree to love but will love in truth, effectively. Then in its turn it must cross the universe to go to God.

Simone Weil (1909-43),
Simone Weil Reader

He showed me a little thing, the size of a hazelnut,
in the palm of my hand, and it was round as a ball.
I looked at it with my mind's eye and thought,
'What can this be?'
And answer came, 'It is all that is made.'
I marvelled that it could last, for I thought it might
have crumbled to nothing, it was so small.
And the answer came into my mind,
'It lasts and ever shall because God loves it.'
And all things have been through the love of God.

In this little thing I saw three truths.
The first is that God made it.
The second is that God loves it.
The third is that God looks after it.

What is He indeed that is maker and lover
    and keeper?
I cannot find words to tell.
For until I am one with Him
I can never have true rest nor peace.
I can never know it until I am held close to Him
that there is nothing in between.

Julian of Norwich (1342-1420),
Daily Readings with Julian of Norwich

Then I saw a new heaven and a new earth; the first heaven and the first earth had disappeared now, and there was no longer any sea. I saw the holy city and the new Jerusalem coming down from God out of heaven, as beautiful as a bride all dressed for her husband. Then I heard a loud voice call from the throne: 'You see this city? Here God lives among men. He will make his home among them; they shall be his people and he will be their God; his name is God-with-them. He will wipe away all tears from their eyes; there will be no more death, and no more mourning or sadness. The world of the past has gone.'

Revelation 21:1-4

And I said to the man who stood at
    the gate of the year
Give me a light that I may tread safely
    into the unknown
And he replied
    Go out into the Darkness
    and put your hand into the hand of God
    That shall be to you better than light
    and safer than a known way.

Louise M. Haskins (1875-1957)
'The Gate of the Year'

And when we have fallen, through frailty or blindness, then our courteous Lord touches us, stirs and calls us. And then he wills that we should see our wretchedness and humbly acknowledge it. But it is not his will that we should stay like this, nor does he will that we should busy ourselves too much with self-accusation; nor is it his will that we should despise ourselves. But he wills that we should quickly turn to him.

He is quick to clasp us to himself, for we are his joy and his delight, and he is our salvation and our life.

Julian of Norwich (1342-1420)
Daily Readings with Julian of Norwich

The nearer you go to God, the nearer he will come to you.

James 4:8

Life
is a precious thing
to me

and a little thing:

my life is a little thing,
when it will end here
is God's secret

And the world
is a little thing

like a hazelnut
in his-her hand —
but it is in his ever-keeping,
it is in his ever-loving,
it is in his ever-making,

how should any thing be amiss?

Yes, all shall be well,
and all will be well,
and thou shalt see thyself
that all manner of thing
shall be well.

Kind friends,

I pray God grant you
all your good wishes,
desires, and dreams —
it is all in the choosing,
it is all in the asking.

J. Jandra,
from Julian (a play based on the life of Julian of
Norwich)

The contemplative life has nothing to tell you except to reassure
you and say that if you dare to penetrate your own silence and
dare to advance without fear into the solitude of your own
heart…you will truly recover the light and capacity to understand

what is beyond words and beyond explanations because it is too close to be explained.

Thomas Merton (1915-68),
The Monastic Journey

The word within a word, unable to speak a word
Swaddled with darkness. In the juvescence
    of the year
Came Christ the tiger.

T.S. Eliot (1888-1965),
'Gerontion'

This inner 'I' which is always alone, is always universal: for in this inmost 'I' my own solitude meets the solitude of every other man and the solitude of God....It is only this inmost and solitary 'I' that truly loves with the love and the spirit of Christ. This 'I' is Christ Himself living in us; and we, in Him, living in the Father.

Thomas Merton (1915-68),
Disputed Questions

You must give up your old way of life; you must put aside your old self, which gets corrupted by following illusory desires. Your mind must be renewed by a spiritual revolution, so that you can put on the new self that has been created in God's way, in the goodness and holiness of the truth.

Ephesians 4:22-4

There was a time, within living memory, when semi-literate country people would down their tools and flock to hear their chapel choirs sing Handel's *Messiah* or Haydn's *Creation*. Now, with the chapels closed, they leave their combine-harvesters to sit in listless apathy in front of the video. The death of the spiritual has caused the fragmentation of community and the erosion of culture.

'Turning and turning in the widening gyre

154

The falcon cannot hear the falconer;
Things fall apart; the centre cannot hold;'

(Yeats)
Andrew Symons,
Christian Meditation by Those Who Practice It

It is a great thing, this reading of the Scriptures! For it is not possible ever to exhaust the mind of the Scriptures. It is a well that has no bottom.

St John Chrysostom (AD 347-407)

O Love, where dost thou lead
Upon what travels fares our caravan?
By Hedjar Desert shall thy footsteps speed
The longest journey since the world began.
Treading love's path so long
Under such heavy burdens did I bow
At last my chastened heart has grown so strong
No task, no pain, can bend my spirit now.

Princess Zebu'n Nisa,
'The Diwan of Zebu'n-Nisa'

Man's primary task is to penetrate within and there discover himself. Whoever has not found himself within himself has not yet found God; and whoever has not found God within himself has not yet found himself. No one finds himself apart from God, and no one finds God apart from himself.

God is he who is at the heart of all, at the origin of all, at the origin even of the utterance of that 'Thou' with which I address him. So long as anyone has not penetrated to that inner source from which diversity itself originates, he is merely cherishing the external idols which he has created on his own petty scale.

Henri Le Saux/Abhishiktananda (1910-73),
The Man and his Teachings

You will never know real mercy for the failings of others until

155

you know and realize that you have the same failings in your own soul.

St Bernard of Clairvaux (1091-1153),
The Classics of Western Spirituality

Where before God he is all alone,
where with God he is all alone,
where in God he is all alone,
where from God he is all alone,
where all alone is He Who Is, —

Chandogya Upanishad

From the unreal lead me to the real,
from darkness lead me to light,
from the mortal lead me to the immortal.

Baihadarmnyaka Upanishad

This is crucial: as long as we pray only when and how we want to, our life of prayer is bound to be unreal. It will run in fits and starts. The slightest upset — even a toothache — will be enough to destroy the whole edifice of our prayer-life.

'You must strip your prayers,' the novice-master told me. You must simply deintellectualise. Put yourself in front of Jesus as a poor man: not with any big ideas, but with living faith. Remain motionless in an act of love before the Father. Don't try to reach God with your understanding; that is impossible. Reach him in love; that is possible.

Carlo Carretto (1910-89),
Letters from the Desert

O thou who art at home
Deep in my heart
Let me lose myself in thee
Deep in my heart.

from a song of the Jewish Talmud

I desired often to know what was our Lord's meaning. And fifteen years after and more, I was answered in inward understanding, saying, 'Would you know your Lord's meaning in this? Learn it well. Love was his meaning. Who showed it to you? Love. What did he show you? Love. Why did he show you? For love. Hold fast to this, and you shall learn and know more about love, but you will never need to know or understand about anything else for ever and ever.' Thus did I learn that love was our Lord's meaning.

Julian of Norwich (1342-1420),
Daily Readings with Julian of Norwich

To go to Rome
great the effort, little the gain,
you will not find there the King you seek
unless you bring Him with you.

Anonymous Irish monk (ninth century)

I can neither read nor write, and I have absolutely no regrets for this. However, I do possess one book, which there is no need to open because it is never shut, a book not written by human hands, which can neither get dirty, nor can it be lost or torn. This book of mine is always wide open, and also always new; it is the book of the interior of my heart.

An Indian sage in conversation with
Henri Le Saux/Abhishiktananda (1910-73),
The Secret of Arunachala

These are only hints and guesses,
Hints followed by guesses; and the rest
Is prayer, observance, discipline, thought and
    action.
The hint half guessed, the gift half understood is
Incarnation.

T.S. Eliot (1888-1965),
Four Quartets

157

What an impossible fellow I am [thought the renegade priest at the point of his death] and how useless. I have done nothing for anybody. I might just as well have never lived....He felt only an immense disappointment because he had to go to God empty-handed, with nothing done at all. It seemed to him at that moment that it would have been quite easy to have been a saint. It would only have needed a little self-restraint and a little courage. He felt like someone who had missed happiness by seconds at an appointed place. He knew now that at the end there was only one thing that counted — to be a saint.

Graham Greene (1904-91),
The Power and the Glory

Come then, my love,
my lovely one, come.
My dove, hiding in the clefts of the rock,
in the coverts of the cliff,
show me your face,
let me hear your voice;
for your voice is sweet
and your face is beautiful.

Song of Songs 2:13

Since no creature whatsoever or any of its actions and abilities can conform or can attain to that which is God, therefore must the soul be stripped of all things created and of its own actions and abilities — namely of its understanding, liking and feeling, — so that when all that is unlike God and unconformed to Him is cast out, the soul may receive the likeness of God; and nothing will then remain in it that is not the will of God and it will thus be transformed in God.

St John of the Cross (1542-91)

The longest way to God,
the indirect,
lies through the intellect.
The shortest way lies through the heart.

Here is my journey's end
and here its start.

Angelus Silesius (1624-77),
The Enlightened Heart

It was the Christians in the Greek city of Thessalonica who
received St Paul's directive:
Be joyful always:
pray continually:
give thanks whatever happens;
for this is what God in Christ wills for you.

1 Thessalonians 5:16-18

We do not
appropriate Christ
for our use.
We do not change him,
but he changes us.
We do not grasp him,
but he grasps us.

Jürgen Moltmann

The Bible speaks of God as a 'consuming fire' and equally the
contemplative tradition of India describes the knowledge of God
in a similar fashion. When a man has once even glimpsed it, it is
all up with him. He can no longer rest content with the world of
signs; he has to plunge himself into the Flame.

Henri Le Saux/Abhishiktananda (1910-73),
The Secret of Arunachala

Among all creatures, the highest and the lowest, there is not one
that remotely resembles God. Yet we naturally persist in confusing
Him with creatures, seeing Him alongside them, as one of them
in fact, albeit the mightiest and greatest. God transcends the
intellect and is inaccessible to it. How far-reaching the consequences of this truth. God Himself is 'night to the soul' in this life

159

and man, rational finite man, is 'towards' this inaccessible one
and can find fulfillment only in him.

Ruth Burrows,
Ascent to Love

Everyone who drinks of this water
will thirst again, but whoever
drinks of the water that I shall give him
will never thirst;
the water that I shall give him
will become in him a spring of water
welling up to eternal life.

John 4:13-14

Where have you hidden yourself, O my beloved?
You leave me in my groanings.
Shy as the deer you have fled away
leaving me wounded.
I ran after you crying, but you were gone!

St John of the Cross (1542-91),
Collected Works of St John of the Cross

I am no longer trying for perfection by my own efforts....I want
only the perfection that comes through faith in Christ and is from
God and based on faith....
All I can say is that I forget the past and I strain ahead for what
is still to come; I am racing for the finish for the prize to which
God calls us upwards to receive in Christ Jesus....
If there is some point on which you see things differently, God
will make it clear to you; meanwhile let us go forward on the road
that has brought us to where we are.

Philippians 3:9, 13-15, 16

The fullness
of joy
is to behold

God in
everything.

Julian of Norwich (1342-1420),
Revelations of Divine Love

The desert traveller begins to realize by experience that not only did God not abandon him or her, but also that he is closer than ever, shedding his light even more brightly. It is a stronger light. Though he is closer than ever, it may feel like darkness. We may suffer because of our own impurities, our own weakness. Like the heat of the desert, the light of God burns away these impurities until we can see his presence.

Stephen J. Rossetti,
I Am Awake: Discovering Prayer

If I have all the eloquence of men or of angels but speak without love, I am simply a gong booming or a cymbal clashing. If I have the gift of prophecy, understanding all the mysteries there are and knowing everything, and if I have faith in all its fullness to move mountains, but without love, then I am nothing at all....
There are three things that last: faith, hope, and love; and the greatest of these is love.

1 Corinthians 13:1-3, 13

He who binds to himself a joy
Does the winged life destroy,
But he who kisses the joy as it flies
Lives in eternity's surprise.

William Blake (1757-1827),
Songs of innocence

My children, mark me, I pray you. Know! God loves my soul so much that his very life and being depend upon his loving me

161

whether he would or not. To stop God loving me would be to rob him of his Godhood.

Meister Eckhart (1260-1327),
Sermons and Treatises

The spiritual path, therefore, is a return to the source of our being. The journey is one of silence for it is in the depth of silence, in the receptive void of our consciousness that God speaks. We continue to pay attention to our external self when the God of our consciousness is made up of ideas, words, feelings, reassuring formulas; such a God is a man-made idol. We are still self-centred when religion is used to protect us against the voice of silence which is the language of the true God. In fact our well-meant personal, inner dialogue is often a spiritual screen hiding the divine presence. Words can be an invasion of our intimacy with God.

François C. Gerard (1924-91),
Going on a Journey

The journey into the inner self is not just the important one, it is the only one. We need to listen to the sound beyond the silence.

W.B. Yeats (1865-1939),
Sayings of Yeats

For the heart of this nation has grown coarse, their ears are dull of hearing, and they have shut their eyes, for fear they should see with their eyes, hear with their ears, understand with their heart, and be converted and be healed by me. But happy are your eyes because they see, your ears because they hear!

Matthew 13:15-16

Yet another elder said: If you see a young monk by his own will climbing up into heaven, take him by the foot and throw him to the ground, because what he is doing is not good for him.

Thomas Merton (1915-68),
Wisdom of the Desert

O you who were created for union with God himself and whom he is ever attracting to himself, what are you doing with your precious lives, with your time? You are labouring for nothingness and all you think you possess is pure misery. O terrible human blindness. So great a light about you and you do not see it, so clear a voice sounding and you do not hear it.

St John of the Cross (1542-91),
'Spiritual Canticle 39'

Religious experience at its roots is experience of an unconditional and unrestricted being in love. But what we are in love with remains something that we have to find out.

Bernard Lonergan (1904-84),
Collected Works

He who believes himself to be far advanced in the spiritual life has not even made a good beginning.

Bishop Jean-Pierre Campus (1582-1652)

They who wait on the Lord shall renew their strength
They shall mount up with eagle's wings
They shall run and not be weary
They shall walk and not faint.

Isaiah 40:31

A contemplative must at some time go into the desert, but he must not go there to escape others, but in order to find them in God. It is dangerous to seek solitude 'merely because you happen to like to be alone.'

William H. Shannon,
Thomas Merton's Dark Path

A good (spiritual) traveller has no fixed plans and is not intent upon arriving.

Lao Tzu (570-490 BC),
Tao Te Ching

We are Easter people and 'alleluia' is our song.

St Augustine (AD 354-430),
The Classics of Western Spirituality

If a man wishes to be sure of the road he treads on, he must close his eyes and walk in the dark.

St John of the Cross (1542-91),
Collected Works of St John of the Cross

Like the deer that yearns for running streams,
     so my soul is yearning for you my God.
My soul is thirsting for God, the God of my life;
     when can I enter and see the face of God?
My tears have become my bread, by night, by day, as I
     heard it said
     all the day long: 'Where is your God?'

Psalm 41:1-4

To come to a knowledge you have not, you must come by a way you know not.

St John of the Cross (1542-91),
Collected Works of St John of the Cross

God is a pure nothing,
     concealed in now and here:
the less you reach for him,
     the more he will appear.

Angelus Silesius (1624-77),
The Enlightened Heart

Are you seeking God? You would not be seeking Him if you had not already found him.

> Blaise Pascal (1623-62),
> *Pensées*

Go not outside, return into yourself; the Truth dwells in the inner person.

> St Augustine (AD 354-430),
> *The Classics of Western Spirituality*

Listen, listen to me, and you will have good things to eat and rich food to enjoy. Pay attention, come to me; listen, and your soul will live.

> Isaiah 55:3

Joy is the gigantic secret of the Christian.

> G.K. Chesterton (1874-1936),
> *Orthodoxy*

In spiritual things, as in every great undertaking, we must be patient and humble enough to start slowly. It is said that the professional mountain guides in Switzerland can always spot novice climbers. They start out too fast. The experienced mountaineer climbs very slowly, but avoids fatigue and eventually reaches the summit. In setting a rule of prayer, therefore, strive for a standard you are sure you can easily maintain. After adhering to a very modest goal faithfully for many months, you may consider raising it. Most likely you will find that what seemed easy in advance proves, over the long haul, to be difficult. Someone has said: a little thing is a little thing, but *faithfulness* in a little thing is a big thing.

> John Jay Hughes,
> *Praying in Silence*

Look after me, God, I take shelter in you.

Psalm 16:1

When the disciple is ready the teacher appears.

Old adage

I am the light of the world; anyone who follows me will not be walking in the dark; he will have the light of life.

John 8:12

God is eternally pregnant.

Meister Eckhart (1260-1327),
Sermons and Treatises

And the Lord went before them by day in a pillar of a cloud, to lead them the way; and by night in a pillar of fire, to give them light.

Exodus 13:21

As the body is clad in clothes,
and the flesh in the skin,
and the bones in the flesh,
and the heart in the whole,
so are we clothed,
body and soul,
in the goodness of God,
and enfolded in it.

Julian of Norwich (1342-1420)
Daily Readings with Julian of Norwich

The love of God, unutterable and perfect,
flows into a pure soul the way that light
rushes into a transparent object.
The more love that it finds, the more it gives
itself; so that, as we grow clear and open,

the more complete the joy of heaven is.
And the more souls who resonate together,
   the greater the intensity of their love,
   and, mirror-like, each soul reflects the other.

                   Dante Alighieri (1265-1321),

10
Prayer

To pray is to enter consciously into communion with God or the Source. At its highest peak prayer becomes contemplation. Here it is wordless. It is a merging of human consciousness with the Divine. At the centre of the prayerful state is the stilling of the mind. 'Be still, and know that I am God,' says the psalmist (Psalm 46:10).

Prayerfulness opens up a channel between the soul and God. So there is intercommunion between the human and the Divine. Prayer stems from meditation, for the latter is preparing the ground for the former. Prayer may be conceived of as a descent into the depths of the heart and as a rising towards the Godhead. In the opened heart is the prayer that does not cease.

Bede Griffiths (1907-93),
The Universal Christ

Moments of great calm,
Kneeling before an altar
Of wood in a stone church
In summer, waiting for the God
To speak; the air a staircase
For silence; the sun's light
Ringing me, as though I acted
A great role. And the audiences

Still; all that close throng
Of spirits waiting, as I,
For the message.

Prompt me God;
But not yet. When I speak,
Though it be you who speak
Through me, something is lost.
The meaning is in the waiting.

R.S. Thomas

Properly understood, prayer is a mature act which is essential for
the complete development of the personality. It is the ultimate
integration of the highest faculties of man. It is only in prayer that
we can achieve the complete and harmonious union of body, mind,
and spirit.

Dr Alexis Carrel (1873-1944)

So the divine light of contemplation, when it beats on the soul,
not yet perfectly enlightened, causes spiritual darkness, because
it not only surpasses its strength, but because it blinds it and
deprives it of its natural perceptions....This is the reason why the
illuminating ray of hidden wisdom, when God sends it from
Himself into the soul not yet transformed, produces thick darkness
in the understanding....The soul, by reason of its impurity, suffers
exceedingly when the divine light really shines upon it....

So great are the weakness and impurity of the soul that the
hand of God, so soft and gentle, is felt to be so heavy and
oppressive, though neither pressing nor resting on it, but merely
touching it, and that, too, most mercifully; for He touches the soul
not to chastise it, but to load it with His graces.

St John of the Cross (1542-91).
Collected Works of St John of the Cross

Only prayer reveals the precipitous depths of our poverty. Submission to it involves an awareness of someone else. We are so
poor that even our poverty is not our own: it belongs to the mystery

of God. In prayer we drink the dregs of our poverty, professing the richness engendered of someone else: God. The ultimate word of impoverished man is 'Not I, but thou.'

Johannes Baptist Metz,
Poverty of Spirit

At the very beginning of our prayer
Christ wants to kindle in us
what is basic to our prayer —
the childlike awe and trust....

Heidelberg Catechism

We simply need quiet time in the presence of God. Although we want to make all our time, time for God, we will never succeed if we do not reserve a minute, an hour, a morning, a day, a week, a month or whatever period of time for God and him alone. This asks for much discipline and risk taking because we always seem to have something more urgent to do and 'just sitting there' and 'doing nothing' often disturbs us more than it helps. But there is no way around this.

Being useless and silent in the presence of our God belongs to the core of all prayer. In the beginning we often hear our own unruly inner noises more loudly than God's voice. This is at times very hard to tolerate. But slowly, very slowly, we discover that the silent time makes us quiet and deepens our awareness of ourselves and God. Then, very soon, we start missing these moments when we are deprived of them, and before we are fully aware of it an inner momentum has developed that draws us more and more into silence and closer to that still point where God speaks to us.

Henri Nouwen,
Reaching Out

Our prayer...will succeed
only if we lose the very thought
of what we are doing
in the thought of him

170

for whom we are doing it...
We succeed in prayer and in love
when we lose ourselves in both,
and are no longer aware
of how we are praying
or in what manner
we are loving.

Karl Rahner (1904-84),
On Prayer

Let those that are great actives and think to girdle the world with their outward works take note that they would bring far more profit to the Church and be far more pleasing to God if they spent even half this time in abiding with God in prayer....Of a surety they would accomplish more with one piece of work than they now do with a thousand and that with far less labor.

John of the Cross (1542-91)
'Spiritual Canticle 24.3'

In your prayers do not babble as the pagans do, for they think that by using many words they will make themselves heard. Do not be like them; your Father knows what you need before you ask him.

Matthew 6:8

Contemplation is to see and to hear from the heart. It takes us beyond sense perception. It is to relate to things as they are.

All so-called spiritual knowledge is useless if simply retained in the head. It is a waste of time and leads to self-delusion. It is to know about rather than to know. The same is true of theological knowledge. This has to be diverted towards the contemplative experience through meditation, otherwise it remains apart from life and is of no ultimate value.

Contemplative seeing is not selective. It is not processed by the brain nor conditioned by previously held concepts and attitudes. It constitutes a whole way of life, a way to be followed by the true disciple of Jesus. Traditionally, contemplation has been thought of as an Eastern approach to religion. Action in this world

171

has been seen as its opposite and typical of the Western understanding. Today's world requires a marriage of the two, that is, contemplation in action.

Bede Griffths (1907-93),
The Universal Christ

The wish to pray is prayer itself.

Georges Bernanos (1888-1948)

We ruin our life of prayer if we are constantly examining our prayer and seeking the fruit of prayer in a peace that is nothing more than a psychological process. The only thing to seek in contemplative prayer is God; and we seek him successfully when we realize that we cannot find him unless he shows himself to us, and yet at the same time he would not have inspired us to seek him unless we had already found him.

Thomas Merton (1915-68),
Thoughts in Solitude

> The Sage reads the Scriptures,
> meditates on them again and again,
> and discovers Brahman;
> then he puts them aside,
> as one does with the taper
> once the lamp is lit.
>
> *Amritanada Upanishad*

There are various degrees of prayer. The first degree is bodily prayer, consisting for the most part in reading, in standing and in making prostrations.

The second degree is prayer with attention: the intellect becomes accustomed to collecting itself in the hour of prayer, and prays consciously throughout, without distraction. The intellect is focused upon the written words to the point of speaking them as if they were its own.

The third degree is prayer of feeling: the heart is warmed by concentration, so that what hitherto has only been thought now becomes feeling. Where first it was a contrite phrase now it is contrition itself: and what was once petition in words is transformed into a sensation of entire necessity. Whoever has passed through action and thought to true feeling will pray without words, for God is God of the heart.

When the feeling of prayer reaches the point where it becomes continuous, then spiritual prayer may be said to begin. This is the gift of the Holy Spirit praying for us, the last degree of prayer that our intellects can grasp.

But there is, they say, yet another kind of prayer which cannot be comprehended by the intellect, and which goes beyond the limits of consciousness.

Bishop Theophane the Recluse (1815-94),
taken from *Seasons of the Spirit*

For the one who asks, always receives, the one who searches, always finds, the one who knocks will always have the door opened to him.

Luke 11:10

No longer am I
The man I used to be
For I have plucked the fruit
Of this precious tree of life.

As the river flows down the hills
And becomes one with the sea,
So has the weaver's love flowed
To become one with the Lord of Love.

Go deeper and deeper in meditation
To reach the seabed of consciousness.
Through the blessing of my teacher
I have passed beyond the land of death.

Says Kabir: Listen to me friends,
And cast away all your doubts.

173

Make your faith unshakable in the Lord,
And pass beyond the land of death.

Kabir (1440-1518),
'The fruit of the tree'

Mysticism is fire without reflection; it is union with the divine in love. It is the primary source of all life, including religious, artistic and intellectual life. Without it, everything becomes pure and simple technique. Religion becomes a body of techniques of which the scribes and Pharisees are the engineers; it becomes legalistic. Art becomes a body of techniques — be they traditional or innovative — a field of imagination or experiences. Lastly, science becomes a body of techniques of power over Nature.

Anonymous spiritual writer,
Meditations on the Tarot

There is no labour so great as praying to God...prayer hath the travail of a mighty conflict to one's last breath.

Abbot Agathe,
The Desert Fathers

The time may come when the soul will feel its prayer to have dried up completely, and will be bewildered that it should be so. This stage is normally regarded as the beginning of mystical prayer. What is happening is that the soul in its generosity is giving everything it knows to God, and seeking him and him primarily. And he is responding and has come so near that the normal apparatus of the mind cannot interpret the experience until it is adjusted to it. Its receiving set, if we can talk in pictures, is swamped by the strength of the signals it receives, and is not at once (or for a long time) able to tune in sufficiently finely to distinguish these.

The result is that at this stage there is very real suffering on the part of the soul, who wants nothing but God, but can only feel desolation and dismay. This stage of wanting and not perceiving has a further significance in that it serves to strip the soul of everything that would intrude between it and God. For though the soul might think it had given all over to God, it has still to learn that there is much yet to be surrendered. God must be loved not merely primarily but for himself alone; all between has to go.

This night of the senses, as some call it, is due to the loving action of God, for, as we have seen, God is now more obviously taking the initiative, and assuming control. Indeed, he has been doing this all along, as the mystic always recognizes. All is 'of grace,' and without God's prevenient mercy nothing in the life of prayer would be possible. But now his action is more apparent, at least to the outside observer; hitherto it has been hidden. This 'night' lasts for just so long as God wills, and, subjectively, for all the time that the soul needs such purging.

Clifton Wolters,
Introduction to *The Cloud of Unknowing*

Until the end we go to our prayer never really knowing what prayer is, never completely free of the foolishness of striving to possess ourselves even there, in the moment of our self-donation. Until the end the poverty of our prayer is there to lead us to a deeper realization of our total dependency on God's guidance and mercy. It seems that those who give themselves over to prayer are not those who know how to pray, but rather are those who are willing to endure the purifying experience of not knowing how to pray and in this unknowing tasting obscurely yet deeply the divine love that is their life.

James Finley,
The Awakening Call

The way of (contemplative) prayer brings us face to face with the sham and the false self that seeks to live for itself alone and to enjoy the 'consolation of prayer' for its own sake. This 'self' is pure illusion, and ultimately he who lives for and by such an illusion must end either in disgust or in madness.

Thomas Merton (1915-68),
Contemplative Prayer

Do not think that the words of prayer as you say them go up to

God. It is not the words themselves that ascend, it is rather the burning desire of your heart that rises like smoke toward heaven.

Or Ha-Me'ir

How can you define prayer, except by saying that it is love? It is love expressed in speech, and love expressed in silence. To put it another way, prayer is the meeting of two loves: the love of God and our love.

Catherine de Hueck Doherty (1896-1985)
Soul of My Soul

Simone Weil has described prayer as a patient waiting with expectancy. It is a paradox of tension that combines the absence and the presence of God; the already and the not yet; the returning and the going; tender loving possession and the agony of searching for the lost.

George Maloney,
Alone with the Alone

No matter where we happen to be, by prayer we can set up an altar to God in our heart.

St John Chrysostom (AD 347-407)

It is good for us to think of prayer realistically. It would be false to define or limit prayer to constant moments of consolation and clarity. The human heart knows the truth and journey of the inner search. The reality of divine and human intimacy involves suffering and sheer human monotony. We sometimes shy away from the sheer enormity of love; we fear its demands, yet we want its intimacy. Our body repels pain and invites pleasure. Being married to constant novelty does not lead to depth of relationship, rather to shallow roots and poverty of truth.

Speaking of our temptation to abandon prayer for fear of what it may ask of us, Simone Weil wrote: 'Frequently pleasure and pain are just the pretexts used by our mediocre ego to separate our attention from God.' Commenting on this a writer on Weil

176

remarked: 'She grasped that there are three ways by which the human person can reach the fullness of truth: the desire for truth, the constant effort of attention, and obedience to one's personal vocation.' On a concrete level we are told that Weil had an irresistible attraction to the Eucharist. Towards the end of her life she wrote: 'I feel an intense and ever increasing desire for Communion.' Simone Weil never formally became a Christian.

Simone Weil teaches us that on our journey to God in prayer we must want to search for and be found by God. She would encourage us to make our questions about prayer into prayers. 'Lord, help us not to give up on our waiting on you. You understand our feeble efforts. Bless our constancy and our desire. Mary, our Mother, help us to see your Son in the silence of our hearts and in our sisters and brothers. Amen.'

Stephen Cummins,
writing on Simone Weil

Prayer opens us to a closeness with God, the compassionate God we know in Jesus Christ. And the closer we get to God, the closer we get to the people of the world. We find the world at the heart of God. A disciple of Christ does not avoid the pain of the world, but penetrates into its center. The deeper the prayer is, the deeper we enter into solidarity with a suffering world. In solitude this compassionate solidarity grows.

In solitude we realize that the roots of all conflict, war, injustice, cruelty, hatred, jealousy, and envy are deeply anchored in our own hearts. Nothing human is alien to us either. In prayer we assume responsibility for injustice in our self and in the world.

Don Postema,
Space for God

Prayer, for me, used to stand as something separate from other parts of life. But I have come to learn that real prayer is not so much talking to God as just sharing God's presence....Prayer, I have learned, is more my response to God than a matter of my own initiative.

Malcolm Boyd,
Are You Running with Me Jesus?

Pray as you can and do not try to pray as you can't. Take yourself as you can find yourself; start from that.

Dom John Chapman (1865-1933),
Spiritual Letters

This is the psalm of contemplative prayer. Man on the way to the roots of his being, towards his end, his creator, after having passed the first degrees of prayer, after having been purified by the suffering dryness of human pleasure and selfishness, finds himself at the doorway of eternity. His own strength can do nothing.

Carlo Carretto (1910-89),
Letters from the Desert

[Jesus] made the disciples get into the boat and go before him to the other side [of the lake], while he dismissed the crowds. And after he had dismissed the crowds, he went up on the mountain by himself to pray. When evening came, he was alone....And in the fourth watch of the night [between 3 and 6 am] he came to them, walking on the sea.

Matthew 14:22-5 (RSV)

He who has learned to pray has learned the greatest secret of a holy and a happy life.

William Law (1686-1761),
The Classics of Western Spirituality

Many people who have trouble praying regularly have told me that creating a certain place for prayer has been helpful. One woman I know uses part of her son's room while he's off to college. On a table in one corner of the room she keeps a Bible, a hymnbook, a candle, and a cross. Over the table hangs a painting of a quiet nature scene. This space is now used for no other purpose than for prayer and contemplation. She says that every time she walks by that room she is reminded of prayer. Others have said the same thing about the place they have set up. One woman uses a small corner in her bedroom; another sits at her kitchen table, looking out over the backyard at the trees, birds, and flowers.

A group of men who live together have created a space in their basement. When the gas meter reader came through and asked 'What's this?' he was surprised to hear, 'This is our prayer room.' One person I know cleared out a long closet and equipped it with an altar, kneeling bench, candle, Bible, and a few books. Another found her private bathroom to be the quietest place for prayer!

The familiarity of one place constantly used for prayer helps settle us into prayer faster and saves our minds from curious wandering. The surroundings can reinforce the prayerful intention of the time we are spending in that place. Our roommates or family members will also become aware that when we are in that place we are not to be disturbed. Such a place can become precious to a husband and wife. Children will gradually sense that this is a valuable space and join in prayer as a natural part of their environment. We need to make space for God in our hearts, but also in our time and in our surroundings.

Don Postema,
Space for God

I understand that prayer (and those lives given to it) is the energy by which God unites the world to himself.

Marilyn Bendzwell

If you desire to stand surrendered before God, then you are standing there. It needs absolutely nothing else. Prayer is the last thing we should feel discouraged about. It concerns nobody except God always longing to give Himself in love — and my own decision. And that too is God's 'who works in us to will and effect.' In a very true sense there is nothing more to say about prayer — 'the simplest thing out.'

Wendy Beckett

Any soul that penetrates within, just by doing so, deepens the Church and the Church's consciousness of herself. It thus calls the Church, as though from depth to depth, in the realization of her own mystery. Each Christian, each group of the faithful, in effect, expresses and manifests in itself the *Una Catholica* as a whole, and in her, the only Lord. That is precisely the irreplaceable role, the very service of contemplatives in the Church.

Henri Le Saux/Abhishiktananda (1910-73),
The Eyes of Light

One believes one has been abandoned by God. In this deeply painful state, prayer becomes true and strong even though it may be as dry as dust. The soul speaks to its God out of its poverty and pain; still more out of its impotence and abjection.

Words become even fewer and barer. One is reduced to silence, but this is a step forward in prayer! It is limitless, whereas every word has a limit. And spiritual greed? Oh, that's always there! It hides under the ashes, but it is less violent, more prudent.

God now again intervenes with his consolation, since it would be impossible to live in that state of abandonment. He returns to encourage the soul with the touch of his gentleness. The soul accepts that touch with gratitude. But it has become so timid through the blows it has received that it dare not ask anything more. Deep down the soul has understood that it must let itself be carried, that it must abandon itself to its Saviour, that alone it can do nothing, that God can do everything.

And if it remains still and motionless, as though bound in the faithfulness of God, it will quickly realise that things have changed, and that its progress, though still painful, is in the right direction. It is in the direction of love! This realisation will come like light after darkness, the midday sun after the dawn.

What matters is to let God get on with it.

Carlo Carretto (1910-89),
Letters from the Desert

Prayer can be real prayer even when it is not filled with bliss. Prayer can be like a slow interior bleeding, in which grief and sorrow make the heart's blood of the inner person trickle away silently into his own unfathomed depths.

Karl Rahner (1904-84),
On Prayer

And when you pray do not imitate the hypocrites: they love to say their prayers standing up in the synagogues and at the street corners for people to see them. I tell you solemnly they have had their reward. But when you pray go to your private room and, when you have shut your door, pray to your Father who is in that secret place, and your Father who sees all that is done in secret will reward you.

Matthew 6:5,6

He who still knows how intensely he is praying has not overcome the bonds of self.

Or Ha-Emet

Prayer itself is God's life within us, God's great dance. When we allow that life to come to ever greater fullness, we become more and more alive, and we begin to live the life of prayer. It is no longer prayer within one's life, but a life that is itself prayer. That is ultimately the aim of Benedictine monasticism.

David Steindl-Rast,
Speaking of Silence

Therefore you must learn a kind of prayer which can be made at all times, which does not divert from outward business, and which princes, kings, prelates, priests, magistrates, soldiers, children, artisans, labourers, women and sick persons, may all perform. This is not the prayer of the head, but prayer of the heart.

It is not a prayer of thought only, because the spirit of man is so bounded that while he thinks on one thing he cannot think on another; but it is the prayer of the heart, which is not at all interrupted by all the occupations of the mind: nothing but irregular affections can interrupt the prayer of the heart: and 'tis almost impossible for the soul which has once tasted God and the sweetness of his love, to relish anything else but him.

Madame Guyon (1648-1717),
A Method of Prayer

SIR THOMAS MORE I believe when statesmen forsake their own private conscience for the sake of their public duties... they lead their country by a short route to chaos. And we shall have my prayers to fall back on.
CARDINAL WOLSEY You'd like that, wouldn't you? To govern the country by prayers?
MORE Yes, I should.
WOLSEY More! You should have been a cleric!
MORE Like yourself, Your Grace?

Robert Bolt,
A Man for All Seasons (Act I)

Without true and deep contemplative aspirations, religion tends in the end to become 'the opium of the people.'

Thomas Merton (1915-68),
Contemplative Prayer

There is just one method...for all: to stand with the attention in the heart; all other things are beside the point and do not lead to the crux of the matter...the essence of the thing is to be established in the remembrance of God, and to walk in his presence...it is important to realize that prayer is always God-given: otherwise we may confuse the gift of grace with some achievement of our own.

Timothy Ware,
The Art of Prayer

Prayer is the key of the morning and the bolt of the evening.

Mahatma Ghandi (1869-1948)

The derivation of the word contemplation can also help to enrich our understanding. It comes from templum, a precinct, a sacred space or edifice, and con-, to view intensely or long. Originally, a temple was not necessarily a building, just a sacred space. Our innermost reality is indeed a sacred place. This place is symbolized in the fire of the burning bush when God says to Moses: 'Take

off your shoes, for the place on which you stand is holy ground.'
God is the sacred place at the centre of every human person.

Madeleine Simon,
Born Contemplative

If we really want to pray we must first learn to listen, for in the
silence of the heart God speaks.

T.S. Eliot (1888-1965)

It is our conviction that the central message of the New Testament
is that there is really only one prayer and that is the prayer of
Christ. It is a prayer that continues in our heart day and night. I
can describe it only as the stream of love that flows constantly
between Jesus and His Father. This stream of love is the Holy
Spirit.

Dom John Main (1926-82),
Moment of Christ

Contemplative prayer takes the presence of the Holy Spirit seriously. Its purpose is to bring his presence into awareness,...and
to bring our hearts into harmony with his voice, so that we allow
the Holy Spirit to speak and to pray within us, and to lend him
our voices and our affections that we may become, as far as
possible, conscious of his prayer in our hearts.

Thomas Merton (1915-68),
Spiritual Direction and Meditation

I went on a weeklong silent retreat. The first night the director of
the retreat told us to set up a daily schedule that included five
hour-long periods of prayer. I went to my room and began setting
up my books, rearranging the furniture. I went to the kitchen to
see whether there was anything to eat. I took a nap — anything
to avoid making that schedule, to avoid entering silence for prayer.
   Gradually I realized that I was afraid. I could hardly pray for
fifteen minutes; now I had to pray for five hours! Then I read a
text assigned to me, words that Haggai had written for people

rebuilding the temple in Jerusalem: 'Take heart....Begin the work, for I am with you, says the Lord of Hosts, and my spirit is present among you. Have no fear' (2:4-5, NEB). I needed that.

Don Postema,
Space for God

There is nothing more powerful than a person praying well.

St John Chyrsostom (AD 347-407)

For example, a contemplative may think that he is seeking God in his prayer when in reality he is seeking the consolations that God sometimes gives with prayer: recollection, interior peace, and the sense of His presence. Clinging to these spiritual experiences can be, even if ever so unconsciously, an attachment to creatures that prevents us from truly seeking God and therefore that blocks the way to true contemplation.

William H.Shannon,
Thomas Merton's Dark Path

Contemplation is not the pleasant reaction to a celestial sunset, nor is it the perpetual twitter of heavenly birdsong. It is not even an emotion. It is the awareness of God, known and loved at the core of one's being.

Clifton Wolters,
Introduction to *The Cloud of Unknowing*

In prayer it is better to have a heart without words, than words without a heart.

John Bunyan (1628-88),
The Works of John Bunyan

In prayer we discover what we already have. You start where you are, you deepen what you already have, and you realize that you are already there. We already have everything, but we don't know it and we don't experience it. Everything has been given to us in

Christ. All we need is to experience what we already possess.

The whole thing boils down to giving ourselves in prayer a chance to realize that we have what we seek. We don't have to rush after it. It is there all the time, and if we give it time, it will make itself known to us.

Thomas Merton (1915-68),
Monastic Studies Issue 7 (1969)

Enter into the inner chamber of your mind. Shut out all things save God and whatever may aid you in seeking God; and having barred the door of your chamber, seek him.

St Anselm of Canterbury (1033-1109),
Anselm of Canterbury

God gives prayer to the man who prays.

John Climacus (AD 570-649),
The Classics of Western Spirituality

Let no one think, my fellow Christians, that only priests and monks need to pray without ceasing, and not laypeople. No, no: every Christian without exception ought to dwell always in prayer...the Name of God must be remembered in prayer as often as one draws breath.

Gregory Palamas (1296-1359),
Writings from the Philokalia

The biggest problem in prayer is how to 'let go and let God.'

Glen Clark,
I Will Lift Up My Eyes

'Faith is prayer to God' [said Dr Zimmerman], 'the silent prayer which a man carries in his heart, his secret with God, which he entrusts to God in the hour of his need.'

Sholom Asch (1880-1957),
'A passage in the night' (Part II)

185

More things are wrought by prayer than the world dreams of.

Alfred Lord Tennyson (1809-92),
Best Loved Religious Poems

Our part in prayer is to try to raise our minds and hearts to God, to spend time making the effort. Trying to pray is prayer, and it is very good prayer. The will to try is also His gift.

Basil Hume,
To Be A Pilgrim

There is but one road which reaches God and that is prayer. If anyone shows you another you are being deceived.

St Teresa of Avila (1515-82),
The Collected Works of St Teresa of Avila

If in your heart you make
a manger for his birth,
then God will once again
become a child on earth.

Angelus Silesius (1624-77),
taken from *The Enlightened Heart*

11
The Human Condition and Grace

Our capacity for discontent
let me observe
is in proportion to our desires;
that is in proportion to the intensity
of our attachments
to things of this world.

Thomas Mann (1875-1955),
Century Classics

There are, besides the gifts of the head, also those of the heart, which are no whit less important, although they may easily be overlooked because in such cases the head is often the weaker organ. And yet people of this kind sometimes contribute more to the well-being of society, and are more valuable than those with other talents.

C.G. Jung (1875-1961),
The Development of Personality

Indeed you love truth in the heart.
Then in the secret of my heart
teach me wisdom.
O purify me then I shall be clean.

O wash me, I shall be whiter than
snow....

A pure heart create for me, O God.
Put a steadfast spirit within me.
Do not cast me away from your presence
nor deprive me of your Holy Spirit.

Psalm 51:8-9,12-13

When your heart no longer burns with love, many others will die
of the cold.

François Mauriac (1885-1970)

Why no! I never thought other than
That God is that great absence
In our lives, the empty silence
Within, the place where we go
Seeking, not in hope to
Arrive or find. He keeps the Interstices
In our knowledge, the darkness
Between stars. His are the echoes
We follow, the footprints he has just
Left. We put our hands in
His side hoping to find
it warm. We look at people
And places as though he had looked
At them, too; but miss the reflection.

R.S. Thomas,
taken from Miraculous Simplicity:
Essays on R.S. Thomas

If we are to pray in the spirit of Christ, we cannot turn our backs
on the suffering of others. Prayer demands that we love our fellow
humans; we have no choice. It can make prayer extremely
dangerous, for example, in situations where humanity is system-
atically suppressed and people are forced to live as though no
bonds of allegiance existed between them. This need for humanity

urges Christians today to adopt a positive attitude towards prayer.

We must pray not just for the poor and unfortunate but with them. This contradicts our instinctive tendency to avoid the company of those who are unhappy or suffering. If we pray 'in his spirit' we can afford to be despised by those who consider themselves to be intelligent and enlightened; but not by those who are disconsolate, suffering or oppressed. And this means that prayer is of necessity political and influential....

Hence we must take care not to let our prayers turn into a eulogistic evasion of what really matters, serving merely to lift the apathy from our souls and our indifference and lack of sympathy towards other people's suffering....A mature attitude towards prayer presupposes the readiness to assume responsibility....

The qualities of this liberating, edifying God to whom we pray must be visible in our conduct and attitudes.

Johannes Baptist Metz,
The Courage to Pray

Be patient and wait for the Lord to act;
Don't be worried about those who prosper
Or those who succeed in their evil plans.
Don't give in to worry or anger;
 it only leads to trouble.
Those who trust in the Lord
 will possess the land,
But the wicked will be driven out.

Psalm 37:7-9

Let us never forget that the ordinary way to contemplation lies through a desert without trees and without beauty and without water. The spirit enters a wilderness and travels blindly in directions that seem to lead away from vision, away from God, away from all fulfillment and joy. It may become almost impossible to believe that this road goes anywhere at all, except to a desolation full of dry bones — the ruin of all our hopes and good intentions.

The prospect of this wilderness is something that so appalls most people that they refuse to enter upon its burning sands and travel among its rocks. They cannot believe that contemplation and sanctity are to be found in a desolation where there is no food and no shelter and no refreshment for their imagination and intellect and for the desires of their nature.

Thomas Merton (1915-68),
New Seeds of Contemplation

Peace is every step
The shining red sun is my heart
Each flower smiles with me
How green, how fresh all that grows
How cool the wind blows
Peace is every step
It turns the endless path to joy.

Thich Nhat Hanh,
Peace Is Every Step

Lead, Kindly Light, amid the encircling gloom,
  Lead Thou me on!
The night is dark, and I am far from home —
  Lead Thou me on!
Keep Thou my feet; I do not ask to see
The distant scene, — one step enough for me.

I was not ever thus, nor pray'd that Thou
  Shouldst lead me on.
I loved to choose and see my path; but now
  Lead Thou me on!
I loved the garish day, and spite of fears,
Pride ruled my will: remember not past years.

So long Thy power hath blest me, sure it still
  Will lead me on
O'er moor and fen, o'er crag and torrent, till
  The night is gone;

190

And with the morn those angel faces smile
Which I have loved long since, and lost awhile.

John Henry Newman (1801-90),
World's Great Religious Poetry

When he was at dinner in the house it happened that a number of tax collectors and sinners came to sit at the table with Jesus and his disciples. When the Pharisees saw this, they said to his disciples 'Why does your master eat with tax collectors and sinners?' When he heard this he replied, 'It is not the healthy who need a doctor but the sick. Go and learn the meaning of the words: "What I want is mercy not sacrifice." And indeed I did not come to call the virtuous but sinners.'

Matthew 9:10-13

I knew
you not
My Lord
because
I still
desired to
know and
delight
in things.

St John of the Cross (1542-91),
Collected Works of St John of the Cross

To walk on the waters, that is the vocation of the Christian. With no human support, in pure faith, in hope and pure charity. With no feeling, sometimes, simply keeping one's eyes raised to God.

Raissa Maritain (1883-1960)
Raissa's Journal,

God, take me by Your hand, I shall follow You dutifully, and not resist too much. I shall evade none of the tempests life has in store for me, I shall try to face it all as best I can. But now and then

191

grant me a short respite. I shall never again assume, in my innocence, that any peace that comes my way will be eternal. I shall accept all the inevitable tumult and struggle. I delight in warmth and security, but I shall not rebel if I have to suffer cold, should You so decree. I shall follow wherever Your hand leads me and shall try not to be afraid.

I shall try to spread some of my warmth, of my genuine love for others, wherever I go. But we shouldn't boast of our love for others. We cannot be sure that it really exists. I don't want to be anything special, I only want to try to be true to that in me which seeks to fulfil its promise. I sometimes imagine that I long for the seclusion of a nunnery. But I know that I must seek You amongst people, out in the world.

Etty Hillesum (1914-43),
An Interrupted Life

> You whom I brought from the confines of the earth
> and called from the ends of the world;
> You to whom I said, you are my servant,
> I have chosen you not rejected you.
> Do not be afraid, for I am with you;
> stop being anxious and watchful....
>
> for I your God am holding you by the right hand;
> I tell you, 'Do not be afraid. I will help you.'

Isaiah 41:9-10,13

He who has a *why* to live can bear with almost any *how*.

Friedrich Wilhelm Nietzsche (1852-1933),
Nietzsche Reader

The sun is shining, the sky is deep blue, there is a lovely breeze and I'm longing — so longing — for everything. To talk, for freedom, for friends, to be alone. And I do so long...to cry! I feel as if I'm going to burst, and I know that it would get better with crying; but I can't, I'm restless, I go from one room to the other, breathe through the crack of a closed window, feel my heart beating, as if it is saying, 'Can't you satisfy my longings at last?' I believe that it's Spring within me, I feel that Spring is awakening, I feel it in my whole body and soul. It is an effort to behave normally, I feel utterly confused, don't know what to read, what to write, what to do, I only know that I am longing.

Anne Frank (1929-45),
The Diary of Anne Frank

Her faith the awful face of God
Brightens and blinds with either light;
Her footsteps fall where late he trod;
She sinks in roaring voids of night;
Cries to her Lord in black despair,
And knows, yet knows not, he is there.

Robert Hugh Benson (1871-1914),
The Teresian Contemplative

If only there were evil people somewhere insidiously committing evil deeds, and it was necessary only to separate them from the rest of us and destroy them. But the line dividing good and evil cuts through the heart of every human being, and who is willing to destroy a piece of his own heart?...Socrates taught us know thyself.

Alexander Solzhenitsyn,
The Gulag Archipelago

I believe in the sun even when it is not shining.
I believe in love even when I cannot feel it.
I believe in God, even when he is silent.

Written on a wall in Cologne
by a Jewish Prisoner

I cannot understand my own behaviour. I fail to carry out the things I want to do and I find myself doing the very things I hate....

The fact is, I know of nothing good living in me — living, that

193

is, in my unspiritual self — for though the will to do what is good is in me, the performance is not.

Romans 7:15,18

Let nothing
disturb you,
nothing afright
you: all passes
away. God only
shall stay:
patience wins all,
who has God
lacks nothing for
God is his all.

St Teresa of Avila (1515-82),
The Collected Works of St Teresa of Avila

The Roman captain asks Lavinia, a young Christian, why she is willing to die as a martyr.

THE CAPTAIN Are you then going to die for nothing?
LAVINIA Yes: that is the wonderful thing. It is since all the
    stories and dreams have gone that I have now no doubt at all
    that I must die for something greater than dreams or stories.
THE CAPTAIN But for what?
LAVINIA I don't know. If it were for anything small enough to
    know, it would be too small to die for. I think I'm going to die
    for God. Nothing else is real enough to die for.

George Bernard Shaw (1856-1950),
Androcles and the Lion (Act II)

His state was divine, yet he did not cling to his equality with God but emptied himself to assume the condition of a slave and became as men are.

Philippians 2:6-7

I do dimly perceive that whilst everything around me is ever changing, ever dying, there is underlying all that change a living power that is changeless, that holds all together, that creates, dissolves, and recreates. That informing power or spirit is God. And since nothing else that I see merely through the senses can or will persist, He alone is.

And is this power benevolent or malevolent? I see it as purely benevolent. For I can see that in the midst of death life persists, in the midst of untruth truth persists, in the midst of darkness light persists. Hence I gather that God is Life, Truth, Light. He is Love. He is the Supreme Good.

Mahatma Gandhi (1869-1948),
My Religion

It is God's will for us that
we should possess
an Interior Castle,
against which the storms of
life may beat without being
able to disturb
the serene quiet within.

Evelyn Underhill (1875-1941)

O Lord support us all the day long, till the shades lengthen and the evening comes, and the busy world is hushed, and the fever of life is over, and our work is done. Then in His mercy may He give us a safe lodging, and a holy rest and peace at the last.

John Henry Newman (1801-1890),
Sermon (1834)

I myself will pasture my sheep. I myself will show them where to rest — it is God who speaks. I shall look for the lost one, bring back the stray, bandage the wounded and make the weak strong. I shall watch over the fat and healthy. I shall be a true shepherd to them.

Ezekiel 34:15-16

Terrible ordeal in silent prayer. Felt all the bitterness of death. God asks of me more than my life: to accept living death, existence in a barren desert. That is giving more than one's soul. *Amaritudo amarissima*. Tortured, sobbing, I felt at the end, as it were, a faint whisper coming from the Lord. As if he were saying to me, 'It is I, Jesus. You will find me again. Yes, you will do my will. Yes, you will accept it. Yes, you will be with me.' The relief, the appeasement in which this prayer ended. But this oraison is all my life now. And death is proposed to me at every instant on God's side. I can accept it — and enter into the world of Jesus — or refuse it and begin to live the life of this world.

Raissa Maritain (1883-1960),
Raissa's Journal

There is no single definition of holiness: there are dozens, hundreds. But there is one I am particularly fond of; being holy means getting up immediately every time you fall, with humility and joy. It doesn't mean never falling into sin. It means being able to say, 'Yes, Lord, I have fallen a thousand times. But thanks to you I have got up again a thousand and one times.' That's all. I like thinking about that.

Helder Camara,
Archbishop of Recife, Brazil

God has created me to do Him some definite service. He has committed some work to me which He has not committed to another. I have my mission; I may never know it in this life, but I shall be told it in the next. I am a link in a chain, a bond of connection between persons. He has not created me for naught. I shall do good — I shall do His work.

If I am in sickness, my sickness may serve Him, in perplexity, my perplexity may serve Him. He does nothing in vain. He knows what He is about. He may take away my friends. He may throw me among strangers. He may make me feel desolate, make my spirits sink, hide my future from me — still he knows what he is about.

John Henry Newman (1801-1890),
'Cardinal Newman's prayer'

The Lord is compassion and love, slow to anger and rich in mercy. His wrath will come to an end. He will not be angry for ever. He does not treat us according to our sins, nor repay us according to our faults.

Psalm 103:8-10

> Darkness shall
> not frighten us
> or distress wear
> us out; we will
> go on waiting,
> watching and
> praying until the
> star rises.

Fr Alfred Delp (1907-45),
The Prison Meditations of Father Delp

The Journey of a thousand miles begins with the first step.

Lao Tzu (570-490 BC),
Tao Te Ching

JOAN Do you think you can frighten me by telling me that I am alone? France is alone; and God is alone; and what is my loneliness before the loneliness of my country and my God?…Well, my loneliness shall be my strength too: it is better to be alone with God: His friendship will not fail me, nor His counsel, nor His love. In His strength I will dare, and dare, and dare, until I die.

George Bernard Shaw (1856-1950),
Saint Joan (Scene V)

Lord, all that I long for is known to you.
My sighing is no secret from you.
My heart is throbbing, my strength deserting me.
The light of my eyes itself has left me.

Psalm 38:9-10

The experience of God's love and the experience of our weaknesses are correlative. These are the two poles that God works with as he gradually frees us from immature ways of relating to him. The experience of our desperate need for God's healing is the measure in which we experience his infinite mercy. The deeper the experience of God's mercy, the more compassion we will have for others....

The work of following Christ is like working with a psychotherapist who has a clear insight into what is wrong with us. With incredible accuracy, God puts his finger on exactly the spot that needs attention at this precise time in our spiritual growth. If we are hanging on to one last shred of possessiveness, he comes along and says, often through some person or event, 'Won't you give this to me?'

Thomas Keating,
Invitation to Love

Come to me all you who labour and are overburdened, and I will give you rest. Shoulder my yoke and learn from me, for I am gentle and humble in heart, and you will find rest for your souls. Yes, my yoke is easy and my burden light.

Matthew 11:28-30

During the period of the Desert Fathers, there was a pietistic sect called the Messalians. These were people who had an overly spiritualised approach to prayer and considered manual work condemnable for a monk. Some of the monks of this sect went to see Abba Lucius. The old man asked them, 'What is your manual work?' They said, 'We do not touch manual work but as the Apostle says, we pray without ceasing.'

The old man asked them if they did not eat and they replied they did. So he said to them, 'When you are eating who prays for you then?' Again he asked them if they did not sleep and they replied they did. And he said to them, 'When you are asleep, who prays for you then?' They could not find any answer to give him.

He said to them, 'Forgive me, but you do not act as you speak. I will show you how, while doing my manual work, I pray without interruption. I sit down with God, soaking my reeds and plaiting

198

my ropes, and I say, "God, have mercy on me; according to your great goodness and according to the multitude of your mercies, save me from my sins.'" So he asked them if this were not prayer and they replied it was.

Henri Nouwen,
The Way of the Heart

Abbot Pastor said that Abbot John the Dwarf had prayed to the Lord and the Lord had taken away all his passions....And in this condition he went to one of the elders and said: You see before you a man who is completely at rest and has no more temptations. The elder said: Go and pray to the Lord to command some struggle to be stirred up in you, for the soul is matured only in battles. And when the temptations started up again he did not pray that the struggle be taken away from him, but only said: Lord, give me strength to get through the fight.

Thomas Merton (1915-68),
Wisdom of the Desert

O Lord, you have shown me my end,
how short is the length of my days.
Now I know how fleeting is my life.
You have given me a short span of days;
my life is as nothing in your sight.
A mere breath, the one who stood so firm;
a mere shadow, the one who passes by;
a mere breath, the hoarded riches,
and who will take them, no one knows.
And now, Lord, what is there to wait for?
In you rests all my hope.
Set me free from the taunt of the fool.
I was silent, not opening my lips,
because this was all your doing.
Take away your scourge from me.
I am crushed by the blows of your hand.
You punish our sins and correct us;
like a moth you devour all we treasure.
Human life is no more than a breath;

O Lord, hear my prayer.
O Lord, turn your ear to my cry.
Do not be deaf to my tears.
In your house I am a passing guest,
a pilgrim, like all forebears.
Look away that I may breathe again
before I depart to be no more.

Psalm 39:1-13

At the beginning of our times together, I said I would begin at the end. What I would end by saying is 'begin.' If you would like to. All you have to do is to want to begin. It is beginning a journey, an adventure, that takes one to the very depths of one's humanity. It is amazing what resources you will find on the way to help you to persevere if you simply begin. Then keep on beginning and never think of yourself, as a meditator, as anything other than a beginner. The only other basic advice is always to keep it simple. We have a tendency to try to complicate things, and meditation is as simple as it sounds. Begin simply and keep it simple. It is very helpful, I think, to feel part of a community because of the communion that meditation naturally creates.

Laurence Freeman,
Short Span of Days

There is no need to travel to Rome or Jerusalem to search for him: but turn your thoughts into your own soul where he is hidden, and seek him there...Jesus is the treasure hidden in your soul. If you could find him in your soul, and your soul in him, I am sure that you would gladly give up the love of all earthly things in order to have him. Jesus sleeps spiritually in your heart as he once slept bodily in the ship with his disciples. But they, fearing to perish, awoke him, and he quickly saved them from the tempest. Therefore rouse him as they did by prayer, and wake him with the loud cry of your desire, and he will quickly rise and help you.

Walter Hilton (1300-96),
The Ladder of Perfection

Come now, let us reason together,
      says the Lord:
though your sins are like scarlet,
      they shall be as white as snow;
though they are red like crimson,
      they shall become like wool.

Isaiah 1:18

There is only one unhappiness, and that is not to be one of the Saints.

Leon Bloy (1846-1917),
The Woman Who Was Poor

Until one is committed, there is hesitancy, the chance to draw back, always ineffectiveness. Concerning acts of initiative (and creation) there is one elementary truth the ignorance of which kills countless ideas and splendid plans: that the moment one definitely commits oneself then Providence moves too.

All sorts of things occur to help one that would never otherwise have occurred. A whole stream of events issues from the decision, raising in one's favor all manner of unforeseen incidents and meetings and material assistance which no one could have dreamt would come their way.

Whatever you can do, or dream you can, begin it. Boldness has genius, power and magic in it. Begin it now.

Johann Wolfgang von Goethe (1749-1832),
Goethe: His Life and Writings

Sometimes it happens that this interior helplessness is a sign of real progress in the interior life — for it makes us depend more completely and peacefully on the mercy of God.

Thomas Merton (1915-68),
Thoughts in Solitude

O God, listen to my prayer, do not hide from my pleading, attend to me and reply. With my cares I cannot rest.

201

Oh that I had wings like a dove to fly away and be at rest. So I would escape far away and take refuge in the desert. I would hasten to find a shelter from the raging wind, from the destructive storm.

As for me I will cry to God and the Lord will save me.

Psalm 55:2-3,6-8,17

Blessed be Jesus who is always near in times of stress. Even when we cannot feel his presence he is close.

Jesus said within my heart, 'I will never leave you either in happiness or distress. I will always be there to help you and watch over you. Nothing in heaven or earth can part you from me.'

'When you are quiet and still I can speak to your heart.'

Margery Kempe (1364-1436),
taken from The Joy of the Saints

I know the path: it is straight and narrow. It is like the edge of a sword. I rejoice to walk on it. I weep when I slip. God's word is: 'He who strives never perishes.' I have implicit faith in that promise. Though, therefore, from my weakness I fail a thousand times, I shall not lose faith.

Mahatma Gandhi (1869-1948),
My Religion

In short, mysticism opens up a new layer of psychic life which is bitter and unpleasant because of its unfamiliarity. But when the eye of love becomes accustomed to the dark, it perceives that the darkness is light and the void is plentitude.

William Johnston,
The Inner Eye of Love

God creates out of nothing. Wonderful, you say. Yes, to be sure, but He does what is still more wonderful: He makes saints out of sinners.

Søren Kierkegaard (1813-55),
Journals and Papers

Modern investigators of miraculous history have solemnly admitted that a characteristic of the great saints is their power of 'levitation.' They might go further; a characteristic of the great saints is their power of levity. Angels can fly because they can take themselves lightly.

G.K. Chesterton (1874-1926)

Our problem is not that we take refuge from action in spiritual things, but that we take refuge from spiritual things in action.

Monica Furlong

We may not look at pleasure to go to heaven in featherbeds. It is not the way; for Our Lord Himself went thither with great pain and by many tribulations.

St Thomas More (1478-1535),
The Complete Works of St Thomas More

The Cross, the Cross
Goes deeper in than we know,
Deeper into life;
Right to the marrow
And through the bone.

D.H. Lawrence (1885-1930)

Holy Spirit,
giving life to all life,
moving all creatures,
root of all things,
washing them clean,

203

wiping out their mistakes,
healing their wounds,
you are our true life,
luminous, wonderful,
awakening the heart
from its ancient sleep.

Hildegard of Bingen (1098-1179)

Let me seek, then, the gift of silence, and poverty, and solitude, where everything I touch is turned into prayer: where the sky is my prayer, the birds are my prayer, the wind in the trees is my prayer, for God is all in all.

Thomas Merton (1915-1968)
Thoughts in Solitude

Your silence draws me like some enchanted scent. I do not know if my house is in order. It matters not, nor does time, for night and day I go in search of thee. I cannot rest.

Catherine de Hueck Doherty (1896-1985)
Journey Inward

12
Hope...Never Give Up

Love is not love
Which alters when it alteration finds,
Or bends with the remover to remove:
O, no! It is an ever-fixed mark
That looks on tempests and is never shaken.

William Shakespeare (1564-1616),
Sonnet 116

Our prayer brings great joy and gladness to our Lord. He wants it and awaits it.

By his grace he can make us as like him in inward being as we are in outward form. This is his blessed will.

So he says this, 'Pray inwardly, even though you feel no joy in it. For it does good, though you feel nothing, see nothing, yes, even though you think you cannot pray. For when you are dry and empty, sick and weak, your prayers please me, though there be little enough to please you. All believing prayer is precious to me.'

God accepts the goodwill and work of his servants, no matter how we feel.

It pleases God that by the help of his grace we should work away at our praying and our living, directing all our powers to

him until in the fullness of joy we have him whom we seek —
Jesus.

Julian of Norwich (1342-1420),
taken from *The Joy of the Saints*

> For your love is better than life.
> My lips will speak your praise.
> On my bed I remember you,
> On you I muse through the night,
> for you have been my help,
> In the shadow of your wings I rejoice.
> My soul clings to you,
> your right hand holds me fast.

Psalm 63:4,7-9

And so diligently persevere until you feel joy in it. For in the beginning it is usual to feel nothing but a kind of darkness about your mind, or as it were, a cloud of unknowing. You will seem to know nothing and to feel nothing except a naked intent toward God in the depths of your being. Try as you might, this darkness and this cloud will remain between you and God. You will feel frustrated, for your mind will be unable to grasp God, and your heart will not relish the delight of God's love.

But learn to be at home in this darkness. Return to it as often as you can, letting your spirit cry out to one whom you love. For if in this life, you hope to feel and see God in all reality it must be within this darkness and this cloud. But if you strive to fix your love on God forgetting all else, which is the work of contemplation I have urged you to begin, I am confident that God's goodness will bring you to a deep experience of the Divine Godhead.

Anon (fourteenth century),
The Cloud of Unknowing

November 21, 1943 ...after this Sunday comes Advent, with all the happy memories for you and me....Life in a prison cell reminds me a great deal of Advent — one waits and hopes and potters about, but in the end what we do is of little consequence, for the door is shut and can only be opened from the outside.

Dietrich Bonhoeffer (1906-45),
The Cost of Discipleship

In God alone is my soul at rest,
my help comes from him.
He alone is my rock, my stronghold, my fortress:
I stand firm.

Psalm 62:2-3

How long must I wait?
God knows.
He can give himself to you overnight,
you can also wait twenty years...

One day he will come.
Once in the stillness...
you will know...

Not from a book
or the word of someone else,
but through him.

Romano Guardini (1885-1968),
'You will know'

Has not man a hard destiny upon earth,
and are not his days like the days of a hireling?
Like a slave who longs for the shadow,
and like a hireling who looks for his wages...

Oh that my words were written!
Oh that they were inscribed in a book!
Oh that with an iron pen and lead
they were graven in the rock for ever!

My foot has held fast to his steps;
I have kept his way and have not turned aside...

For I know that my Redeemer lives,
and at last he will stand upon the earth.
And after my skin has been thus destroyed,
then from my flesh I shall see God,
whom I shall see on my side,
and my eyes shall behold, and not another.
My heart faints within me in expectation!

Job 7:1-2,19:23-4,23:11,19:25-7

Now this point is very important and very practical. Not infrequently one meets people who have spent years in dryness, in inner suffering, in darkness. Their meditation is sleepy and uncomfortable and seems like a waste of time: they think they are doing nothing. But the tiny flame of love is burning quietly in the depths of their being; the loving knowledge is there in secret; their experience is profoundly mystical.

This will seem less strange as we reflect that human love is often just the same. It grows secretly at night when no one is watching like the seed scattered upon the ground. Then one morning we wake up — and there it is! Quite often it is only in moments of separation and death that we advert to the depth of our own love. Or again human love may at first be filled with rapturous joy; but the lean and fallow years have to come.

William Johnston,
The Inner Eye of Love

Whither shall I go from thy spirit? or whither shall
    I flee from thy presence?
    If I ascend up into heaven, thou art there: if I make
        my bed in hell, behold, thou art there.
    If I take the wings of the morning, and dwell in the
        uppermost parts of the sea;
        Even there shall thy hand lead me, and thy right
        hand shall hold me.

208

If I say, Surely the darkness shall cover me; even
    the night shall be light about me.
  Yea, the darkness hideth not from thee; but the
    night shineth as the day: the darkness and the light
    are both alike to thee.

Psalm 139:7-12.

Perhaps if there is any truth that I would hope that new contemplatives would discover, it is what I have just mentioned. How may people enter the spiritual path with enthusiasm! They taste the milk of God and are excited. But when the milk disappears, so does their enthusiasm. Did not Jesus say it would be like that, seed sown on rocky ground? They would accept the Word joyfully but would have no roots and falter (cf. Mk 4:16-17).

Stephen J. Rossetti.
I Am Awake: Discovering Prayer

I waited, I waited for the Lord
and he stooped down to me,
he heard my cry.
He drew me from the deadly pit, from the
    miry clay,
He set my feet upon a rock
and made my footsteps firm.
Happy the man who has placed his trust in
    the Lord.

Psalm 40:1-3

The more the spirit in its forward progress arrives, by ever greater and more perfect application, at an understanding of what it means to know these realities, and comes closer and closer to contemplation, the more it sees that the divine nature is invisible. Having left behind all appearances, not only those which are perceived by the senses, but also those which the intelligence believes itself to apprehend, it enters further and further within until, with great struggle of the spirit, it penetrates to the Invisible and Unknowable, and there sees God.

St Gregory of Nyssa (AD 335-94),
The Classics of Western Spirituality

Do Not Fear
what may happen tomorrow.
The same loving Father
who cares for you today
Will care for you tomorrow
    and everyday.
Either He will shield you
    from suffering,
    or He will give you
unfailing strength to bear it.

Be At Peace Then,
    and put aside all anxious
    thoughts and imaginings.

St Francis de Sales (1567-1622),
The Classics of Western Spirituality

Ask, and it will be given you;
Seek, and you will find;
Knock, and it will be opened to you.
For everyone who asks receives,
And he who seeks finds,
And to him who knocks it will be opened.

Matthew 7:7-8

Love in action is a harsh and dreadful thing compared with love in dreams. Love in dreams is greedy for immediate action, rapidly performed and in the sight of all. Men will even give their lives if only the ordeal does not last long but is soon over with all onlooking and applauding as though on the stage. But love is labour and fortitude....Just when you see with horror that in spite

210

of all your efforts you are getting further from your goal instead of nearer to it — at that very moment — you will reach it and behold clearly the miraculous power of the Lord who has been all the time loving and mysteriously guiding you.

Fyodor Dostoevsky (1821-81)
The Brothers Karamazov

You are to step above it with great courage and with determination and with a devout and pleasing stirring of love, and you are to try to pierce that darkness which is above you. You are to strike that thick cloud of unknowing with a sharp dart of longing love; and you are not to retreat no matter what comes to pass.

Anon (fourteenth century),
The Cloud of Unknowing

In the spiritual life there are no tricks and no short cuts....One cannot begin to face the real difficulties of the life of prayer and meditation unless one is first perfectly content to be a beginner and really experience oneself as one who knows little or nothing, and has a desperate need to learn the bare rudiments. Those who think they 'know' from the beginning never, in fact, come to know anything....

We do not want to be beginners. But let us be convinced of the fact that we will never be anything else but beginners, all our life.

Thomas Merton (1915-68),
The Climate of Monastic Prayer

Prayer is like watching for the
Kingfisher. All you can do is
Be where he is likely to appear, and...
Wait.

Ann Lewin,
Candles and Kingfishers

The brothers asked Abba Agathon: Father, which of the virtues

211

of our way of life demands the greatest effort? He said to them: Forgive me, but there is no effort comparable to prayer to God. In fact, whenever you want to pray, hostile demons try to interrupt you. Of course they know that nothing but prayer to God entangles them. Certainly when you undertake any other good work, and persevere in it, you obtain rest. But prayer is a battle all the way to the last breath.

Yushi Nomura,
Sayings from the Desert Fathers

Strengthen all weary hands,
steady all trembling knees
and say to all faint hearts:
Courage, Do not be afraid.
Look. Your God is coming.

Isaiah (25:3-4)

We never need to pray so earnestly as when we cannot lay hold of any pleasure in prayer.

François Fénelon (1651-1715),
Christian Perfection

Pray to God in the storm,
but keep on rowing!

Danish proverb

When forced, as it seems, by thine environment to be utterly disquieted, return with all speed into thy self, staying in discord no longer than thou must. By constant recurrence to the harmony, thou wilt gain more command over it

Marcus Aurelius Antoninus (AD 121-180),
A Biography

Abba Poemen said about Abba Pior that every single day he made a fresh beginning.

Yushi Nomura,
Sayings from the Desert Fathers

A lot of the road to heaven has to be taken at 30 mph.

Evelyn Underhill (1875-1941),
Letters of Evelyn Underhill

During the darkest periods of history, quite often a small number of men and women, scattered throughout the world, have been able to reverse the source of historical evolutions. This was only possible because they hoped beyond all hope. What had been bound for disintegration then entered into the current of a new dynamism.

Roger Schutz,
Living Today for God

Peace I leave with you, my peace I give unto you: not as the world giveth, give I unto you. Let not your heart be troubled, neither let it be afraid.

John 14:27

It is right that you should begin again every day. There is no better way to finish the spiritual life than to be ever beginning it over again, and never to think that you have done enough.

St Francis de Sales (1567-1622),
The Classics of Western Spirituality

The desert, the absence of consolations, is a long and barren part of the spiritual life. In fact, most of the spiritual life is lived in the absence of consolations. Such sweetness is usually the exception and not the rule. If the presence of God is felt only as sweetness, then the contemplative is doomed to a spartan life of dryness and struggle. What is left is a fairly miserable existence of hanging on until God decides to come again.

The contemplative is then on a sort of spiritual merry-go-round. God comes and God goes. We feel good and then he leaves and we hang on until he comes again. One minute we are up and the next we are down. The contemplative life is then an alternating existence of ups and downs.

Obviously, this is not acceptable, nor is it God's design for us. Our God is not so arbitrary nor so harsh with his loved ones. While the life may initially feel like a merry-go-round, the contemplative must move into a deeper way. The movement into the desert is not a call to hang on until God comes again. It is a call to know him in a more profound manner, to experience God in a new way.

Stephen J. Rossetti,
I Am Awake: Discovering Prayer

The soul of one who loves God always swims in joy, always keeps holiday and is always in the mind for singing.

St John of the Cross (1542-91)

I am done with great things and big things, great institutions and big success, and I am for those tiny invisible molecular moral forces that work from individual to individual, creeping through the crannies of the world like so many rootlets, or like the capillary oozing of water, yet which, if you give them time, will rend the hardest monuments of man's pride.

William James (1842-1910),
A letter to Mrs. Henry Whitman

A martyr, a saint, is always made by the design of God, for His love of men, to warn them and to lead them, to bring them back to His ways. A martyrdom is never the design of man; for the true martyr is he who has become the instrument of God, who has lost his will in the will of God, not lost it but found it, for he has found freedom in submission to God. The martyr no longer desires anything for himself, not even the glory of martyrdom.

T.S. Eliot (1888-1965),
Murder in the Cathedral (Interlude)

The gloom of the world is but a shadow.
Behind it, yet within reach, is joy.
There is radiance and glory in the darkness,
Could we but see,
And to see, we have only to look.
I pray that for you, now and forever,
The day breaks and the shadows flee away.

Fra Giovanni (sixteenth century)

In this place of which you say, 'It is a waste'...there shall be heard again the voice of mirth and the voice of gladness, the voice of the bridegroom and the voice of the bride, the voices of those who sing.

Isaiah 33:10-11

Epilogue

I hope that this book of spiritual quotations will have assisted all those who have found the practice of contemplative prayer a way to deepen their own inner spiritual journey.

In a world increasingly aware of the need for silence and stillness, the teaching of the late Benedictine monk John Main (1926-82) on Christian meditation speaks to us today with the authority of a method that is rooted in both Christian tradition and authentic experience. Since his death over 1,000 Christian meditation groups and twenty-two Christian meditation centres have sprung up in forty countries all over the world.

To many people meditation may be an unfamiliar way of prayer despite its ancient place in Christian tradition attested to by this anthology. This traditional way of contemplative prayer renewed in the twentieth century by John Main allows ordinary people to be aware of the seeds of contemplation buried within themselves.

Meditation acknowledges the potential of the 'holiness of all the people of God.' Most meditation groups today are led by lay people. In this renewal of a Christian tradition of prayer there is also great potential for Christians of all denominations to meet in common faith. Indeed people of all religions can meet in their common humanity by meditating together.

In 1991, meditators from around the world met at the John Main Seminar in New Harmony, Indiana, USA. Led by the late Benedictine monk Bede Griffiths they formed The World Community for Christian Meditation. The WCCM is composed of meditators, meditation groups and the Christian Meditation Centres in cities around the world. A quarterly newsletter unites this spiritual family and retreats or conferences are held regularly in all the participating countries. For further information write to: The World Community for Christian Meditation, International Centre, 23 Kensington Square, London W8 5HN. Tel: 0171 937 4679; fax: 0171 937 6790.

Acknowledgements to Publishers

The editor acknowledges with gratitude the courtesy of those publishers, or other organisations and individuals who have given special permission for me to use extracts from their copyright material, and my thanks are also due to others whose copyright material has been included in this book. Thank you to the following for permissions.

Abbaye de Bellefontaine: *Nil Sorsky: Life and Writings;* Ahmedabad-Navajivan: *My Religion* by Mahatma Gandhi; Alba House: *Journey Inward* by Catherine de Hueck Doherty; Amity House: *Open Mind, Open Heart* by Thomas Keating; AMS Press: *Marcus Aurelius Antoninus, Roman Emperor* by Henry D. Sedgwick; Sri Aurobindo Ashram: *The Evolution of Spiritual Man* by Sri Aurobindo; Ave Maria Press: *The Awakening Call* by James Finley; Ayer Co. Publishers: *Children of Abraham* by Sholom Asch;

Banner of Truth: *The Works of John Bunyan,* edited by George Offor; Bantam Books: *Peace is Every Step* by Thich Nhat Hahn; Bloodaxe Books: *Kneeling* by R.S. Thomas; Burns and Oates: *The Eternal Year* by Karl Rahner;

Carol Publishing Group for *The Contemplative Life* by· Joel S. Goldsmith; Casterman-Tournai: *Ermites du Saccidananda* by Henry Le Saux/Abhishiktananda; Catholic Truth Society: *The Prayer of Silence* by Maurice Nassan; *The Curé of Ars* by Mary Elizabeth Hebert; *Praying in Silence* by John Jay Hughes; Chiron Publications: *Behold Woman* by Carrin Dunne; Cistercian Publications: *The Climate of Monastic Prayer* by Thomas Merton; *The Sayings of the Desert Fathers* translated by Benedicta Ward; *Contemplative Prayer* by Thomas Merton; Citadel Press: *The Contemplative Life* by Joel S. Goldsmith; Claretian Publications: *A Wider Vision* by Gerry Pierse; A. Clark Books: *Seeds of the Desert: Legacy of Charles de Foucauld* by René Voillaume;

Anthony Clarke, Publishers, Wheathampstead, Hertfordshire: *Seeds of Contemplation* by Thomas Merton; Clark City Press: *Hua Hu Ching;* James S. Clark: *A Method of Prayer* by Madame Guyon; T. & T. Clark Ltd: *A Karl Barth Reader* edited by R. J. Erler and R. Marquard; Collier-Macmillan: *Varieties of Religious Experience* by William James; Wm Collins and Sons Ltd: *Reaching Out* by Henri Nouwen; *Christian Mysticism Today* by William Johnston; *Something Beautiful for God* by Mother Teresa; *The Hymn of the Universe* by Pierre Teilhard de Chardin; Contemplative Ministries: *Alone with the Alone* by George A. Maloney; Cowley Publications: *Contemplating Now* by Monica Furlong; CRC Publications: *Space for God: The Study and Practice of Prayer and Spirituality* by Don Postema; *Cross Currents Magazine*: Article by Kallistos Ware, Volume 24; Crossroad: *Seeking the Face of God* by William Shannon; *A Listening Heart* by David Steindl-Rast; *The Courage to Pray* by Johannes Baptist Metz: *The Prison Meditations of Father Delp* by Alfred Delp;

Darton, Longman & Todd: *Ascent to Truth* by Ruth Burrows; *In Search of the Beyond, Letters from the Desert* by Carlo Carretto; *Encountering the Depths* by Mother Mary Clare; *The Selfless Self, Light Within* by Laurence Freeman; *The Way of Paradox* by Cyprian Smith; *The Universal Christ* by Bede Griffiths; *Moment of Christ, The Present Christ, Community of Love, The Inner Christ, Word Made Flesh* by John Main; *Ascent to Love* by Ruth Burrows; *The Way of the Heart* by Henri Nouwen; *Born Contemplative* by Madeleine Simon; *Teach Us to Pray* by André Louf; *Community and Growth* by Jean Vanier; J.M. Dent and Sons Ltd: *The Mystical Element of Religion* by Friedrich von Hügel; Dimension Books Inc.: *Christian Meditation By Those Who Practice It,* edited by Paul T. Harris; *The Eyes of Light* by Henri Le Saux/Abhishiktananda; Doubleday and Co.: *The Gospels Without Myth* by Louis Evely; *Thomas Merton on Mysticism* by Raymond Bailey; *Desert Wisdom — Sayings from the Desert Fathers* by Yushi Nomura; Dover Publications Inc.: *The Analects of Confucius,* translated by J. Legge; Duckworth Publishing: *Sayings of W.B. Yeats* edited by Joseph Spence;
Editions de Seuil: *The Hymn of the Universe* by Pierre Teilhard de Chardin (1957); Element Books Inc.: *Meditations on the Tarot* (Anonymous); *Meister Eckhart: Sermons and Treatises; Invitation*

to Love by Thomas Keating;

Faber & Faber Ltd: *The Art of Prayer: An Orthodox Anthology* edited by Kadoubovsky and Palmer; *Early Fathers from the Philokala* edited by Kadoubovsky and Palmer; *T.S. Eliot, the Complete Poems and Plays*; *Writings from the Philokalia on Prayer of the Heart* edited by Kadoubovsky and Palmer, *The Silence of St Thomas* by Joseph Pieper; Farrar, Straus and Giroux Inc.: *Thomas Merton's Dark Path* by William H. Shannon; *The Road to Joy: Letters to New and Old Friends* by Thomas Merton; *The Hidden Ground of Love (Letters)* by Thomas Merton; Fowler Wright Books: *Being A Christian Today* by Ladislaus Boros; Franciscan Press: *Teach Us to Pray* by André Louf (USA);

François C. Gerard Estate: *Going on a Journey* by François C. Gerard; Grail Publications: *Living from Within* by Philippa Craig;

Harcourt Brace and Co.: *The Little Prince* by Antoine de Saint-Exupéry (USA); *The Heart of Matter* by Pierre Teilhard de Chardin; *The Sign of Jonas* by Thomas Merton; *The Seven-Storey Mountain* by Thomas Merton; *Toward the Future* by Pierre Teilhard de Chardin; *Murder in the Cathedral* by T.S. Eliot; HarperCollins: *Hymn of the Universe* and *The Divine Milieu* by Pierre Teilhard de Chardin; *Pilgrim at Tinker Creek* by Annie Dillard; *Christian Perfection* by François Fénelon, edited by Charles E. Whiston; *The Inner Eye of Love* by William Johnston; *Silent Music* by William Johnston; *Life Together* by Dietrich Bonhoeffer; *Reaching Out* by Henri Nouwen; *Meister Eckhart: A Modern Translation* by Raymond Bernard Blakney; *Celebration of Discipline* by Richard Foster; *The Gulag Archipelago* by Alexander Solzhenitsyn; *Enneads* by Plotinus; *Persian Mystic and Writer* by Jalal al din Rumi; HarperCollins-Fount: *Letters to Contemplatives* by William Johnston (UK); Harper San Francisco: *Celebration of Discipline* by Richard Foster; Harvill Books: *The World of Silence* by Max Picard; *Poems of St John of the Cross*; William Heinemann: *The Little Prince* by Antoine de Saint-Exupéry (UK); Helicon Press: *Living Today for God* by Roger Schutz; David Higham Associates: *The Power and the Glory* by Graham Greene; Hodder & Stoughton: *The Way of the Ascetics* by Tito Colliander, *Celebration of Discipline* by Richard Foster

(UK); Holt, Rinehart & Winston: *Are You Running With Me Jesus?* by Malcolm Boyd;

Institute of Carmelite Studies: *The Collected Works of St John of the Cross* translated by Kieran Kavanaugh and Otilio Rodriguez; *Story of a Soul* translated by John Clarke; *The Collected Works of St Teresa of Avila, Vol. II* translated by Kieran Kavanaugh and Otilio Rodriguez; ISPCK Books: *In Spirit and Truth, Prayer, The Secret of Arunachala* by Henri Le Saux, *Abhishiktananda, His Life Told Through His Letters* edited by James Stuart, *The Man and His Teaching* edited by Sister Vandana;

A. James Ltd.: *I Will Lift Up My Eyes* by Glen Clark; J. Janda from the play Julian; Julian Press: *The Cloud of Unknowing* translated by Ira Progoff;

P.J. Kenedy: *The Autobiography of St Thérèse of Lisieux;* A.A. Knopf: *Thoughts in Solitude* by Thomas Merton; *Disputed Questions* by Thomas Merton; *The Prophet* by Kahlil Gibran, *Markings* by Dag Hammerskjöld;

Ann Lewin: *Candles and Kingfishers* by Ann Lewin; Liepman AG: *The Diary of Anne Frank*; Liturgical Press: *On Prayer* by Karl Rahner; *Spiritual Direction and Meditation* by Thomas Merton; Longman: *The Letters of Evelyn Underhill* edited by Charles Williams; Lyrebird Press: *The Way of Life According to Lao Tzu;*

Macmillan, London: *One Hundred Poems of Kabir* translated by Rabindranath Tagore; *The Power of Prayer* edited by W.P. Paterson and David Russell; *The World's Great Religious Poetry* edited by Caroline Mills Hill; *Christian Zen* by William Johnston (UK); Madonna House Publications: *Poustinia* by Catherine de Hueck Doherty; Magi Books: *Raissa's Journal* by Raissa Maritain; George A. Maloney: *Alone with the Alone* by George Maloney; Manoj Das: *The Evolution of Spiritual Man* by Sri Aurobindo; Marshall Pickering: *The Road to Joy: Letters to New and Old Friends* by Thomas Merton; *The Hidden Ground of Love (Letters)* by Thomas Merton; Edwin Mellen Press: *Anselm of Canterbury* edited by Hopkins and Richardson; The Merton

Legacy Trust: *The Monastic Journey* by Thomas Merton; Methuen and Co.: *Lamps of Fire* by Peter of Alcántara; *Christian Mysticism* by Dean William R. Inge; Modern Library: *The Complete Poetry of William Blake; Francis Thompson Complete Poems*; Moyer Bell: *Simone Weil Reader* edited by George A. Panichas; MSG House: *Goethe: His Life and Writings*; John Murray: *On Zen* by Dai-o-Kokushi;

New Directions: *Seeds of Contemplation* by Thomas Merton; *Wisdom of the Desert* by Thomas Merton; *Zen and the Birds of Appetite* by Thomas Merton; *New Seeds of Contemplation* by Thomas Merton; Nilgiri Press: *St Teresa of Avila*, translated by Eknath Easwaran; *Meditation and God Makes the Rivers to Flow* by Eknath Easwaran, copyright 1991, Nilgiri Press, Tomares, CA 94971; Novalis: *Short Span of Days* by Laurence Freeman;

Orbis Books: *Letters to Contemplatives* by William Johnston (USA);Oxford University Press: *Browning Poetical Works* edited by Norman H. MacKenzie; *The Poems of Gerard Manley Hopkins* edited by Norman H. MacKenzie;

Pantheon Books: *Tales of the Hasidim* by Martin Buber; Pantheon Books 1994/Washington Square Press 1985: *An Interrupted Life: The Diaries of Etty Hillesum* translated by Arno Pomerans (USA); Paulist Press: *Classics of Western Spirituality,* Editor in Chief John Farina; *Are We Losing the Faith?* by Gregory Baum; *The Other Side of Silence* by Morton Kelsey; *Gratefulness the Heart of Prayer* and *Speaking of Silence* by David Steindl-Rast; *The Way to Contemplation* by Willigis Jager; *I am Awake: Discovering Prayer* by Stephen J. Rossetti; *The Interior Castle* by St Teresa of Avila; *Morning Light* by Jean Sullivan; *Poverty of Spirit* by Johannes Metz; Pendle Hill: *Prayer in the Contemporary World* by Douglas V. Steere; Penguin Books Ltd: *Mysticism: A Study and an Anthology* by F.C. Happold; *The Brothers Karamazov* by Fyodor Dostoevsky, translated by David Magarsheck; *A Nietzsche Reader* translated by R.J. Hollingdale; *The Ladder of Perfection* by Walter Hilton, translated by Leo Sherley-Price; *The Cloud of Unknowing* edited and translated by Clifton Wolters; *Oxyrhynchus Sayings of Jesus on Mysticism* by F.C. Happold; *Twentieth Century Classics* (by Thomas Mann translated by H.T.L. Porter); Pilgrim Press Corp.: *Heidelberg Catechism;* Laurence Pollinger

Ltd: *The Wisdom of the Desert* and *Zen and the Birds of Appetite* by Thomas Merton; Princeton University Press: *Collected Works of C.G. Jung, Vol. 17* edited by G. Adler and R.F. Hall;

Ramakrishna-Vivekananda Centre of New York: *The Gospel of Sri Ramakrishna* translated by Swami Nikhilananda; *Songs of Sri Ramakrishna;* Random House, Inc.: *A Man for All Seasons* by Robert Bolt; *The Brothers Karamazov* by Fyodor Dostoevsky; Random House UK Ltd.: *Small is Beautiful* by E.F. Schumacher; Readers Digest: *Archaeologist Story;* Henry Regnery Co.: *The Lord* by Romano Guardini; Fleming H. Revell Co.: *Best Loved Religious Poems* compiled by James Gilchrist Lawson; Routledge & Kegan Paul: *The Dialogue of St Catherine of Siena* translated by Algar Thorold; *Waiting for God* by Simone Weil;

St Bede's Publications: *Finding Grace at the Centre* by Thomas Keating; *The Life of Prayer and the Way to God* by Mary Clare Vincent; St Vladimir's Seminary Press: *The Way of the Ascetics* by Tito Colliander; SCM Press: *The Cost of Discipleship* by Dietrich Bonhoeffer (UK); Seabury Press: *A Life We Never Dared Hope* For by Roger Schutz; *The Way of the Heart* by Henri Nouwen; Shambala Publications Inc.: *The Way of Chaung Tzu; Tao Te Ching* edited by T. Cleary; Harold Shaw Publications: *The Weather of the Heart* by Madeleine L'Engle; Sheed & Ward: *The Spiritual Letters of Dom John Chapman;* Sheldon Press: *The Silent Life* by Thomas Merton; Simon & Schuster: *The Cost of Discipleship* by Dietrich Bonhoeffer (USA); *Varieties of Religious Experience* by William James; *A Hundred Poems of Kabir* translated by Rabindranath Tagore (USA); SLG Press: *The Face of God* by Gilbert Shaw; *The Letters of St Anthony the Great* translated by Derivas J. Chitty; the Society of Authors: *Androcles and the Lion* by George Bernard Shaw; Society of St Paul: *To Be A Pilgrim* by Cardinal Basil Hume; *SPCK Books: In Spirit and Truth, Prayer by Henri Le Saux;* The *Way of a Pilgrim,* by R.M. French; *Dionysius the Areopagite, On the Divine Names and Mystical Theology* by C.E. Rolt; Sphere Books Ltd.: *Small is Beautiful* by E.F. Schumacher;

Templegate Publishers: *Metropolitan Anthony of Sourozh* in the *Modern Spirituality Series*; *Dietrich Bonhoeffer* in the *Modern*

Sprituality Series; The New Creation in Christ, The Golden String by Bede Griffiths; *St. Therese of Lisieux* in the *Daily Readings Series;Thomas Merton* in the *Modern Spirituality Series; The Joy of the Saints; Julian of Norwich* in the *Daily Readings Series*; Charles E. Tuttle Co. Inc.: *A Flower Does Not Talk* by Zenkai Shibayama;

University of Arkansas Press: *Miraculous Simplicity: Essays on R.S. Thomas;* University of Toronto Press: *Collected Works of Bernard J. Lonergan* edited by Frederick Crowe and Robert Doran; University of Washington Press: *Saint Joan* by George Bernard Shaw;

Viking/Penguin USA: *The Complete Poems of D.H. Lawrence* edited by Vivian de Sola Pinto and Warren Roberts; V.F. Vineeth, *Songs of Solitude;*

Wildwood House Ltd: *Tao Te Ching*; World Community for Christian Meditation: *Woman: Her Intuition for Otherness* by Eileen O'Hea;

Yale University Press: *The Complete Works of Thomas More,* executive editor Richard S. Sylvester

The editor and the publisher would be glad to hear from any copyright holder whom they have been unable to trace. Due acknowledgement will be made in future editions of this book.

Index